CYTOGENETIC DISCREPANCIES AND PEDANTIC PERFORMANCE

A STUDY IN CHILDREN

CHANDRA BAHADUR SINGH DANGI

We would like to dedicate this Research study in Children to the Global Research and Welfare Society, Bhopal along with the Scientific Researchers , Medical and Life Science students who are involved in Clinical Cytogenetic and Teaching Professions.

Contents

Acknowledgements

I took this privilege and pleasure to acknowledge the contribution of so many individuals who have been inspirational and supportive throughout this work undertaken and endowed us with the most precious knowledge to see success in our endeavor.

I am deeply grateful to our benefactor, Dr. Sadhna Kapoor (Chancellor), Shri Siddharth Kapoor (MD) Prof (Dr.) Sudesh Kumar Sohani (Vice-Chancellor), and Dr. B N Singh (Director Management), Ram Krishna Dharmarth Foundation University, Bhopal, (M.P.) for their unwavering and enthusiastic encouragement in bringing out this book, to its zenith.

Throughout its preparation, many well-wishers have given their free help and advice and colleagues who shared their knowledge and insight. In this respect, I especially thank Dr. S. P. Paikray (Group Chairman), Care Pro Bioscience Pvt. Ltd, India, for providing us facilities of scientific laboratory and support for the significant outcome of an investigation.

Many thanks to the Faculty of Science, Ram Krishna Dharmarth Foundation University, Bhopal, (M.P.) for their sincere support, continuous encouragement, which largely contributed to bringing out this publication.

I extend our special thanks to Prof. Shadma Siddiqui (Prof. and Head) School of Paramedical Sciences, SAM Global University, Raisen (M.P.) for editing and writing of this book and efforts in the organizational process for turning the manuscript into book form.

I'm extremely grateful to Dr. Kavita Singh as a co-author, Dr. S.D. Singh as a Illustrate of this book, researchers and publishers, whose books have been widely referred to, and data which were utilized extensively in this book and bring the book in experimental shape.

Prof.(Dr.) Chandra Bahadur Singh Dangi

Foreword

The present study demonstrated the frequency of chromosomal abnormalities in subjects with intellectual disability and control. The rapid progress of the cytogenetic study and the numerous researches conducted under the auspices of cytogenetic abnormalities, render it a difficult task to interpret facts.

Chromosomal abnormalities are an important cause of intellectual disability and their frequency increases with the severity of the intellectual disability. It is concluded that chromosomal studies in children with intellectual disabilities assist in accurate diagnosis and proper prognosis followed by genetic counseling and management rehabilitation.

The e-book "**CYTOGENETIC DISCREPANCIES AND PEDANTIC PERFORMANCE: A study on Children** " by **Prof.(Dr.) C B S Dangi** provides a number of papers that are excellent examples of advanced works applied to relevant problems. This book covers key areas in Conventional cytogenetics, Microarray technologies, Molecular cytogenetics, and Chromosome rearrangements

The contributions by the authors include manipulation of variable and genetic resources of inheritance of a quantitative gene. Chromosome analysis is one of the first approaches to genetic testing and remains a key component of genetic analysis of constitutional and somatic genetic disorders. Numerical or unbalanced structural chromosome abnormalities usually lead to multiple congenital anomalies.

This book forms a valuable addition to the existing body of knowledge and is especially intended for university students and researchers in Cytogenetics, Biotechnology, Genetics, and Gene Therapy.

Prof. Shadma Siddiqui
Dean, School of Paramedical Sciences
SAM Global University, Raisen (M.P.)

Preface

Poor scholastic performance is a symptom, where the child scores poor marks which remain below the class average or backwardness in relation to the average attainment for that age and grade. The underlying cause may be genetic in nature in many cases showing variability in symptoms and genetic defects. Poor scholastic performance may be intellectual disability (ID), which is characterized by significant limitations in both intellectual functioning and adaptive behavior that begin before the age of 18 years, affects neatly 1.5 to 2% of the population in the world. A diagnosis of intellectual disability is usually made when IQ testing reveals an IQ of less than 70, which means that often the diagnosis is not made until late childhood or early adulthood. However, most persons with intellectual disability (ID) are identified early in childhood on the basis of concern about developmental delays, which may include motor, cognitive, and speech delays. Many human genetic disorders are caused by missing or duplicated pieces of genetic material or chromosome, known as a copy number variant (CNV). The limits of resolution were the band widths themselves, typically between 3 and 5 million bases. Karyotyping still has a role in identifying large scale copy number variant disorders and in identifying balanced translocations. Karyotyping is done by many hospital laboratories for diagnosis of genetic disorders. Steady advances in chromosome-banding techniques facilitated the detection of unbalanced rearrangements, including translocations, large deletions or duplications, and supernumerary marker chromosomes.

During the last decade, the learning disability movement has definitely picked up momentum in India, and more and more children with this „invisible handicap" are being identified. There is paucity of epidemiological studies in India to determine the exact prevalence of scholastic backwardness. Moreover, studies are required to better understand genetic basis if any, in different cases of poor scholastic performance among children.

In view of the magnitude of the problem of the poor scholastic children in the society, present research was carried out in the city of Bhopal situated in Central India, in order to study its chromosomal basis. The primary aim has been to delineate new chromosomal variations, if any, in mental deficiency leading to poor scholastic performance in children using the cytogenetic tools.

The magnitude of chromosomal abnormalities in children with Intellectual disability poses a serious health problem in our country and still requires further examinations in diverse populations with varied socio-cultural features in future studies.

CHAPTER I

CYTOGENETIC: AN INTRODUCTION

Learning depends on the relationship and interplay of familial, psychological, educational, social, and economic atmosphere in and around the child. At the individual level child"s optimum cognitive development influences the learning behavior. However, poor academic performance is observed among some children. Academic backwardness in children is a complex issue, having various causes. Furthermore, every child"s problem is unique in nature. Academic performance has become an indicator of the child"s future in a contemporary highly competitive world. Poor academic performance has significant consequences on the child and adolescent potential in our society.

Poor Academic Performance

Poor academic performance may be an intellectual disability (ID), which is characterized by significant limitations in both intellectual functioning and adaptive behavior that begin before the age of 18 years, affecting nearly 1.5 to 2% of the population in the world. A diagnosis of intellectual disability is usually made when IQ testing reveals an IQ of less than 70, which means that often the diagnosis is not made until late childhood or early adulthood. However, most persons with intellectual disability (ID) are identified early in childhood on the basis of concern about developmental delays, which may include motor, cognitive, and speech delays (Mefford. 2012; 2018 a,b; 2019).

Poor academic performance is a symptom, where the child scores poor marks which remain below the class average or backwardness in relation to the average attainment for that age and grade. The underlying cause may be genetic in nature in many cases showing variability in symptoms and genetic defects (Jayaprakash, 2005 Kavita Singh, 2018a,b; 2019).

Human Gene Complement

The human gene complement referred to as 'the genome" is made up of about 3.3 billion bases (6.6 billion base pairs) organized onto 23 pairs of chromosomes involving 22 autosomes and the X and Y sex chromosomes. They contain about 22,000 genes, referred to as "the exome', that comprise 1.5% of all the genetic material, as well as the intergenic DNA which influences gene expression and other regulatory functions, which make up the other 98.5% of genetic material. There is an additional small molecule of DNA (16,569 bases), known as mitochondrial DNA, found within the mitochondria (Satya-Murti *et al.* 2013).

Genetics and Intelligence

The first methodical set of experimental observations can be traced back to Galton"s work in 1865, a year before Mendel"s influential article on the laws of heredity. Galton evaluated the transmission of several traits in families using statistical tools. He concluded that many traits including mental ability are genetically transmitted and normally distributed in the general population (Galton, 1869).

Galton (1876) suggested the twin design and the adoption design and, each of these investigated intelligence (Burks, 1928). The first animal model research on learning and problem solving was also relevant to individual differences in intelligence, most notably the successful selection study of maze-bright and maze dull rats bred initially by Tolman in 1924 and continued by Tryon (McClearn, 1963;). In 1963 a review in the Science of genetic research on intelligence was influential in showing the convergence of evidence from family, twin, and adoption studies pointing to genetic influence (Erlenmeyek and Jarvik, 1963). During the 1960s, environmentalism was beginning to diminish in psychology and the stage was set for increased acceptance of genetic influence on intelligence (Plomin and Spinath, 2004)

Identical twins have identical DNA but differing environmental influences throughout their lives affect which genes are switched on or off. This is called epigenetic modification. A study of 80 pairs of twins ranging in age from 3 to 74 showed that the youngest twins have relatively few epigenetic differences. The number of differences between identical twins increases with age. 50-year-old twins had over 3 times the epigenetic difference that the 3- year-old twins had. Twins who had spent their lives apart (such as those adopted by two different sets of parents at birth) had the greatest difference (Fraga *et al.* 2005).

Genetic Disorders

Many human genetic disorders are caused by missing or duplicated pieces of genetic material or chromosome, known as a copy number variant (CNV). The limits of the resolution were the bandwidths themselves, typically between 3 and 5 million bases (Tharpa 2013 Kavita Singh, 2018a). Karyotyping still has a role in identifying large-scale copy number variant disorders and in identifying balanced translocations. Karyotyping is done by many hospital laboratories for the diagnosis of genetic disorders. Steady advances in chromosome-banding techniques facilitated the detection of unbalanced rearrangements, including translocations, large deletions or duplications, and supernumerary marker chromosomes (Kavita Singh, 2018a,b; 2019). A genetic groundwork of mental deficiency disorders has long been recognized in a subset of cases, with trisomy 21 known as Down"s syndrome detectable by chromosomal studies since 1959 (Lejeune, et al. 1959). Trisomy 21 remains the most important chromosomal cause of intellectual disability. Single-gene causes have also been identified for several intellectual disability syndromes and include both autosomal and X-Linked genes, with the fragile X syndrome being the most common of inherited syndromes caused by a single-gene defect leading to this phenotype in male patients.

Chromosomal Karyotyping

Genetic testing was first introduced as a clinical tool in the 1960s with the advent of chromosomal karyotyping. This test allows the chromosomes to be visualized under a common microscope. Special stains applied to the chromosomes captured in metaphase give each chromosome a characteristic pattern of stripes, or "banding pattern." Most banding pattern tests have a resolution limit of about 550-650 'bands'. Trained professionals can view photographs from banding tests and determine whether all or part of a chromosome is missing, duplicated, or abnormally located. Genetic disorders such as Down syndrome, caused by a duplication of chromosome 21 resulting in 3 copies (Trisomy 21), Turner syndrome, caused by loss of 1 X chromosome (monosomy X), as well as hundreds of other diseases resulting from duplication or deletion of smaller amounts of genetic material could be diagnosed with this technique as long as the change is visible under the microscope. (Butler, 1986).

The minimum size of a disrupted chromosome that can be detected by chromosome banding is approximately 5 to 10 Mb, and such cytogenetically visible rearrangements are responsible for 10 to 15% of cases of intellectual disability (Ropers, 2008). It was soon recognized that some patients with syndromic forms of intellectual disability also had deletions in the same chromosomal region, a finding that resolved the molecular cause of microdeletion syndromes, including the Prader-Willi and Angelman syndromes with deletion of 15qll-ql3 (Butler, 1986), the Williams-Beuren syndrome with deletion of 7qll.23 (Perez Jurado, 1996) and the Smith-Magenis syndrome with deletion of 17pl2 (Smith, 1986). It was also noted that 1 to 3% of patients with autism had a maternally inherited duplication involving 15qll- ql3 (Hogart, 2010 Kavita Singh, 2018a,b; 2019).

Several novel microdeletions have been identified in patients who have an intellectual disability. Heterozygous deletions of 17q21.31, which were described by three groups simultaneously, are associated with moderate-to-severe intellectual disability, hypotonia, facial dysmorphic features, occasional cardiac and renal abnormalities, and seizures (Hunter, N. and May, J. 2003). The deletion is 500 to 650 kb in size and is not detectable by routine karyotyping. All 17q21.31 deletions that have been identified are de novo, and the deletion has never been seen in healthy control subjects. Its prevalence is estimated to be approximately 1 in 16,000 persons.75 Deletions of 15q24 are much rarer, but patients with 15q24micro deletions also have an intellectual disability syndrome with recognizable features. Common features include developmental delay and intellectual disability that are usually moderate to severe (Koolen, 2006; Sharp, 2006; Shaw-Smith, 2006).

Need of the Study

According to Chugh S. (2011) in her NUEPA, occasional paper, nearly 17 percent of the children stopped going to school after losing interest in their studies due to poor comprehension. It has often been observed that poor understanding at the elementary level is the main factor contributing to low comprehension at the secondary level. Researchers have also reported a connection between measures of academic performance in early elementary school and dropout behavior before high school graduation (Boyle et al, 2002; Hunter & May 2003;). They also emphasize the need for examining the causes of dropping out before high school, as many students were observed to be dropping out before Grade X. Those who reach a secondary level with weak academic understanding find it difficult to sustain. Even though they were taking private tuitions, they were still not able to understand Maths and English.

The students, who had dropped out, indicated that their reasons for dropping out include -not being able to identify with what is going on in the classroom; teachers not explaining what needed to be done; teachers going too fast; and insufficient time to complete class assignments. Further, the children felt that they had been put on a schedule with no flexibility and a sense of defeat seemed to have prevailed due to the insensitive attitude of the teachers and other staff members, leaving them with no other alternative but to go away from the school. Intelligence was one of the first human traits to be the target of genetic research even before psychology emerged as a scientific field. The correlation between DNA sequence and behavioral differences such as intelligence is considered causal because DNA variations can lead to behavioral differences but behavioral differences do not change DNA sequences (Deary et al., 2006;). Academic backwardness contributes to school dropout, especially after the primary school years, and should be recognized and remedial measures initiated, in the primary classes themselves for best results (Kamat et al. 1934).

Significance of the Study

In the broad sense, mutations include all changes in the hereditary material. Changes in submicroscopic particles of chromosomes that make up the gene structures, as well as visible structural and numerical changes in chromosomes, are included. Those that can be recognized by observations of organisms must be capable of altering phenotypes. Usually, the term "mutation" is employed by geneticists in a restricted sense to specify only gene changes or point mutations, in contrast to visible chromosome changes. It is not always possible in actual practice, however, to distinguish between point mutations and structural changes. Chromosome deficiencies (deleted segments of chromosomes, for example) can be observed by the light microscope and they are known to occur at the molecular level of magnitude in the genetic material (Kavita Singh, 2018a,b; 2019). The underlying cause of academic backwardness should be identified and the appropriate remedy is given soon so that the academic performance of such children can be made better. Academic underachievement of children is a big concern among parents and teachers in present-day competitive society. Karande, (2005) reported that around 20% of school children have academic backwardness. Factors associated with academic backwardness include physical illnesses, below-average intelligence, learning disorders, attention hyperactivity disorder, and psychiatric disorders (Pratinidhi *et al.* 1992, Mogasale *et al.* 2012). During the last decade, the learning disability movement has picked up momentum in India, and more and more children with this „invisible handicap" are being identified (Kavita Singh, 2018a). There is a paucity of epidemiological studies in India to determine the exact prevalence of academic backwardness. Moreover, studies are required to better understand the genetic basis if any, in different cases of poor academic performance among children.

• • •

CHAPTER II

BIBLIOGRAPHIC REVIEW

This review is an exhaustive survey of literature involving important information of the field of interest concentrating on various latest publications along with those that were classic and pioneering. The review begins with background information and progresses to various facets of the subject involving genetic abnormalities leading to mental deficiency.

Background Information

Formal school education plays a great role in everyone's life. Unsettled poor academic performance poses instant and lifelong unfavorable effects on a child and adolescent's growth and cognitive development. The optimum cognitive development of a child influences his/her learning behavior which is influenced by the interaction of family, society, psychology, education, and economical atmosphere of the child. Poor academic performance is observed among some children.

All traits of an individual are products of heredity and environmental interaction. Individuals with varied genotypes appear differently by exposure to common environmental factors. Interactions of Gene and environment can result in different disease phenotypes and Intellectual abilities. Intelligence was one of the first human traits to be the target of genetic research even before psychology emerged as a scientific field. The correlation between DNA sequence and behavioral differences such as intelligence is considered causal because DNA variations can lead to behavioral differences but behavioral differences do not change DNA sequences (Deary et al., 2006; Academic, 2018 a,b).

Intellectual disability and Poor Academic Performance

The "poor academic performance" is a broad term and defined as one in which a student is not successful in attaining standard performance achievement of a child remaining below the expected for his/her age,(Academic, 2018a,b; 2019). American Association on Mental Retardation (AAMR) and American Psychiatric Association (APA) define mental retardation on the basis of certain formulations developed by them. Poor academic performance may be the result of Intellectual disability characterized by radically sub-average intellectual level, existing concurrently with limitations in two or more of the following adaptive skill areas: communication ability, self-care, social skills, self-direction, community use, health and safety, leisure, home living and work (Luckasson et al. 1992; Kavita Singh, 2018a, b).

> "*The American Psychiatric Association (APA) is responsible for naming, defining, and describing mental disorders. Fifth edition of the Diagnostic and Statistical Manual of Mental Disorders (DSM-5), APA changed the term mental retardation and proposed the new term* ***Intellectual Disability or Intellectual Developmental Disorder.***"

Definition of Concepts

Defining mental retardation remains a challenge and a matter of controversy. Ever since people have been able to distinguish mental retardation from other forms of mental disability, a central theme of definitions has concerned the failure of mentally retarded persons to adapt adequately to their surroundings. Older definitions were couched in terms of adult behavior, and there was a tendency to avoid precise criteria for deciding in borderline instances. Tredgold (1956) defined mental deficiency as a state of incomplete mental development of such a kind and degree that the individual was incapable of adapting himself to the normal environment of his fellows in such a way as to maintain existence independently of supervision, control, or external support. Doll (1953)provided a more specific definition. In addition to the element of social adaptation, he emphasized the emergence of handicap in childhood, its constitutional nature, and its incurability. He considered some criteria generally considered essential to an adequate definition and concept. These involve social incompetence, mental sub-normality, developmentally arrested, obtained at maturity, constitutional origin, and essentially incurable.

Kanner (1943)defined two groups of mentally deficient persons in terms of adult status. His definitions balanced the degree of handicap with the nature of the environment to which the individual is forced to adjust. The one group consists of individuals so markedly deficient in their cognitive, emotional, and constructive conation potentialities that they would stand out as defectives in any existent culture. They would be equally helpless and ill-adapted in a society of savants and a society of savages. They are not only deficient intellectually but deficient in every sphere of lifestyle. The other group involves individuals whose limitations are related to the standards of the particular culture which surrounds them. In less complex, less intellectually centered societies they would have no trouble in attaining and retaining equality of realizable ambitions. Some might even be capable of gaining superiority by assets other than those measured by the intelligence test. They could make successful peasants, hunters, fishermen, tribal dancers. They can, in our society, achieve success as farmhands, factory workers, miners, charwomen. But in our midst, their shortcomings, which would remain unrecognized and therefore non-existent in the awareness of a more primitive cultural body, appear as soon as academic curricula demand completion in spelling, history, geography, long division, and other preparations deemed essential for the tasks of feeding food, and working in a shop. Therefore, it is preferable to speak of such people as intellectually inadequate rather than mentally deficient(KavitaSingh, 2018 a, b).

Definition according to Test Score (IQ)

Many writers have attempted to specify quantitative standards for deciding the mental subnormal levels. The most widely used objective criterion of this sort has been the score obtained on a standardized test of intelligence such as the Stanford-Binet Intelligence Scale or the Wechsler Intelligence Scale for Children (WISC). In 1916, Terman introduced a grouping of abilities according to IQs obtained on the Stanford-Binet (Terman and Merrill,1937). This system became widely used and became the standard classification system (Table 1). An IQ of 70 has gained considerable popularity as a cutoff score for the retarded group (Kavita Singh, 2018 b).

There are several difficulties with these scoring criteria. Because an IQ is simply a score obtained based on a restricted sample of behavior, there are significant limitations as to what can or should be expected of it, even if the tests are perfectly reliable and children are always able to put forth their best efforts.

Furthermore, no cutoff score will ever be adequate to define mental retardation independent of the setting in which the individual finds himself. Different skills and abilities are required at different ages and in different environments. Retardation must therefore be gauged in large part against current environmental demands(Kavita Singh, 2018).

Taman's classification* (1937 S-B distribution)	IQ range	Wechsler's classification (WAIS distribution)#
Very superior (1.33 %)	160-169	Very superior (2.2 %)
	150-159	
	140-149	
	130-139	
Superior (11.3 %)	120-129	Superior (6.7 %)
High average (18.1 %)	110-119	Bright normal (16.1 %)
	100-109	
Normal average (46.5 %)	90-99	Average (50 %)
Low average (14.5 %)	80-89	Dull normal (16.1 %)
Borderline defective (7.6%)	70-79	Borderline (6.7%)
	60-69	Defective (2.2 %)
	50-59	
Mentally defective (0.67%)	40-49	
	30-39	

*Terman and Merril (1937)
Wechsler
Figures in parentheses are percentage of standardization group in each category

Table 1: Distribution of IQ's as per Stanford-Binet and Wechsler tests

Apart from this, the cutoff scores for measures of intellectual function are better recognized than the cutoff scores for measures of adaptive behavior. There is an open agreement in the major diagnostic systems that performance on the intellectual dimension must be approximately two or more standard deviations below the population mean, which translates into an IQ score of 70 or less on measures with a mean of 100 and a standard deviation of 15 (Reschly et al. 2002, Kavita Singh, 2018 a,b; 2019)

Critics of IQ classifications have deplored the fact that IQs are sometimes substantially affected by non-intellectual factors such as language handicaps and emotional barriers, and that individual IQ"s sometimes change markedly over time. Realistically, however, classifications according to IQ, when taken in conjunction with other aspects of behavior, do serve a positive function; adherence to objective standards can minimize unfairness and capriciousness in many situations (Kavita Singh, 2018 a,b; 2019)

Contemporary definitions

Mercer (1973) stated in her writing that most definitions of mental retardation have followed either a pathological or a statistical model. The pathological model is concerned with physiological malfunction and symptoms of disease or defect, normality being the absence of symptoms of pathology. With a statistical model like th3t derived from the intelligence-testing movement, mental retardation is defined as a deviant range on a continuum of intellectual ability, normal status then being regarded as the average or middle range. Mercer further developed the third mode of definition according to a social system perspective, in which "mental retardate" is an achieved social status and mental retardation is the role associated with that status: an individual is retarded only if he has been so labeled in some system of which he is a member. Mental retardation is thus a socially defined role or status, which is different from personal characteristics such as low IQ which can affect the probability that a particular child will be assigned that status and will play that role (Mercer, 1973, Mukherjee and Shignapure, 2016). The American Association on Mental Deficiency defines mental retardation as a significantly sub-average general intellectual function existing concurrently with deficits in adaptive behavior and manifested during the developmental period. As an integral part of the definition, each key term has been defined (Mukherjee and Shignapure, 2016).

Mental Retardation

Mental Retardation is defined as a level of performance concerning etiology. Thus it does not distinguish between retardation associated with psychosocial or polygenic influences and retardation with the biological deficit. Mental retardation is descriptive of current behavior and does not imply prognosis. Prognosis is related more to such factors as associated conditions, motivation, treatment, and training opportunities than to mental retardation itself (Mukherjee and Shignapure, 2016).

Intellectual Functioning

Intellectual Functioning may be assessed by one or more of the standardized tests developed for that purpose.

Significantly Sub-average

Significantly Sub-average refers to the performance that is more than two standard deviations from the mean or average of the tests. On the most frequently used test of intelligence, Stanford-Binet and Wechsler, this represents IQ's of 67 and 69, respectively. It is emphasized that despite current practice a finding of low IQ is never by itself sufficient to make the diagnosis of mental retardation.

Adaptive Behavior

Adaptive Behavior is defined as the effectiveness or degree with which the individual meets the standards of personal independence and social responsibility expected in his age and cultural group. Since these expectations vary from different age groups, deficits of adaptive behavior will vary at different ages (Kavita Singh, 2018 b). In this definition the retarded person is judged in terms of his success with the developmental tasks appropriate for his age: in the preschool period, sensorimotor behaviors assume the greatest importance, while during the school years academic ability is of first interest, and during adulthood economic independence and social recognition. Furthermore, this definition makes it clear that a designation of mental status should be a description of present behavior and implicitly disowns the notion of potential intelligence (Reschly, D.J; Myers, T.G; Hartel, C.R. editors 2002).

Developmental Period

The upper age limit of the developmental period is placed at 18 years.

Classification systems

Mentally Retarded or intellectually disabled individuals comprise a very heterogeneous group both in their behavior and in the causes of their deficiency. Different classification systems have been proposed in the past to bring some order in this disarray. Most systems have approached the problem from one of three viewpoints: severity of the handicap, etiology of the symptoms, and symptom collection (Kavita Singh, 2018 b). These classification systems have not only served the purpose of systematization of theoretical and practical knowledge but also served the purpose of preventive or therapeutic measures and management and counseling. Diagnosis and counseling are continuous processes. Counseling should begin with the diagnosis process; diagnosis should continue throughout the counseling interviews. It is imperative for the professionals engaged in the diagnosis to be involved in counseling. Participation of parents remains important in the counseling process (Stafford and Meyer, 1968)

Classification based on the severity of the symptoms

A practical model of classification is provided by the determination of the degree of intellectual deficiency. For many years the terms *idiot, imbecile*" and *moron* were used to denote abilities roughly in the IQ ranges 0 to 30, 30 to 50, and 50 to 70 respectively. In Great Britain, the term *feebleminded* replaced the term *moron* and similar terms were used in other countries, but all these are now quite out of vogue. The terminology proposed at the 1968 Meeting of the World Health Organization **(WHO, 1968)** has now been generally adopted (Table 2}. This system is a simple one, based on the standard score obtained by the individual on a reliable test of intelligence. It is designed to be taken in conjunction with a classification system of adaptive behavior (Kavita Singh,2018b).

1948 Terminology	1968 Terminology	IQ
Idiot	Profound	0-20
High degree imbecile	Severe	20-35
Low degree imbecile	Moderate	35-50
Feebleminded/moron	Mild	50-70
Borderline	Borderline	70-85

Table 2: WHO Classifications of the Degree of Mental Retardation

Classification based on Etiology

A system that conceptualizes the field of retardation in terms of etiology has several advantages for teaching, research, and prevention. Mental retardation syndromes may be differentiated according to criteria of causation or etiologic factors such as congenital or acquired, hereditary or environmental, primary or secondary forms of mental handicap. The ninth revision of the International Classification of Diseases (Kamat, V. V. 1934, WHO, 1975) recommended by the WHO contains ten etiologic categories for mental retardation (Table3) (https://www.who.int/mental_health).

S.No.	Causal Factors
1.	Infections and intoxications
2.	Trauma and physical agents
3.	Disorders of metabolism, growth or nutrition
4.	Gross brain damage (postnatal)
5.	Diseases or conditions due to unknown prenatal influences
6.	Chromosome abnormalities
7.	Prematurity
8.	Major psychiatric disorder
9.	Psycho-social (environmental) deprivation
10.	Other and unspecified

Table 3: WHO List of Causal Factors of Mental Retardation

This classification system, however, has disadvantages and may be misleading. A deficit can seldom be diagnosed as due exclusively to biology or to life experience since the interplay of both is incessant. The source of a deficit is very often obscured by subsequent experiences. An approach based on etiology should be supplemented by other ways of looking at the child. An observation unit of the mentally retarded child must be built upon a multidisciplinary basis. Medical and clinical genetic etiological diagnosis, highly important in prognosis and prevention, must be supplemented by psychological evaluation with IQ testing, orthopedagogic observation, and broad interest for educational programs adapted to the specific problems of the mentally retarded and their families (WHO, 1968, https://ww.who.int/mental_health).

Additional criteria for Classification

Persons with mental retardation can also be grouped by age, an important criterion in education and longitudinal evaluation. Mainly for purposes of management, mental retardation can also be subdivided according to the biological syndrome. This classification offers advantages for special training and schooling in mentally retarded patients with associated deficits such as blindness, deafness, and spina bifida (Kavita Singh, 2018b).

The classifications described above are not completely adequate and this reflects a lack of both fundamental knowledge on different aspects of mental retardation and the multidisciplinary approach and interest in this difficult field. The mental and cognitive outcome of a developing child is dependent on the combined action of genetic and environmental influences. Plato already made a distinction between nature and nurture. Although it is clear that psychosocial factors are very important in the ultimate mental development, socio-familial deprivation is frequently erroneously presumed to be the sole cause of the mental defect WHO, 1968 https://www.who.int/mental_health).

Causes and Consequences

The causes of poor academic performance can be broadly classified into two groups that involve genetics and environment. The present study exclusively aims to focus on genetic causes of PSP however, discussion on medical and varied environmental factors remains imperative. There may be a genetic basis of various medical problems associated with PSP, and many problems are purely environmental in their origin (Kearsey, M. J, 1998)

Poor scholastic performance (PSP) shows multiple etiologies. Many reasons are responsible for the poor scholastic performance of children involving specific learning disabilities, attention deficit hyperactivity disorder, low IQ level, emotional problems, and psychiatric disorders. Other reasons involve a poor socio-cultural home environment and additional environmental causes. The causes of PSP can be further divided into extrinsic or environmental and intrinsic or individual factors. School difficulty (SD) and learning disability (LD) are two different manifestations of some school-attending children. Former is related to pedagogical difficulties. Apart from diseases and related disabilities, pedagogical difficulties can also pose poor scholastic performance. It is extrinsic in nature with no possibilities of organic impairment (Siqueira and Gurge-Giannetti, 2011). Environmental reasons may infuse lack of interest in studies and distraction among some children may result in disappointment, frustration, low self-esteem, and failure (Karande and Kulkarni, 2005). Emotional causes are also important while considering poor academic inspiration, low self-esteem and lack of sympathy, and unresponsiveness formal education (Blair, 2002; Raver, 2002). Therefore, for a flourishing learning process, numerous cognitive skills associated with proper opportunities are essential (Kavita Singh, 2018b).

Present work exclusively focuses on genetic causes of Poor academic performance hence; this largely involves Mental Deficiency (MD) which is again a developmental disability characterized by sub-mental level or lower than average intelligence of the age of a child. This is chiefly associated with biological causes that may show developmental delay or/and involvement of genes or chromosomes. The modest beginning of the investigation of the genetic basis of mental deficiency started long back in1938 with a preliminary study of patients confined to hospital institutions(Penrose, 1938). In recent years focus was on the identification of smaller and smaller chromosome variations associated with disease (Lucy Raymond and Tarpey, 2006).

Abnormal development of a child that leads to mental retardation may be due to trauma before birth caused by an infection or exposure to alcohol, drugs, or other toxins and trauma during birth caused by deprivation of oxygen or premature delivery of a newborn child. Inherited disorders involve point mutation(s) and gross chromosomal abnormalities. Certain point mutations cause metabolic disorders that lead to mental retardation phenotype such as phenylketonuria (PKU). On the other hand, a chromosomal abnormality such as Down syndrome demonstrates peculiar morphological and abnormal behavioral traits. The average IQ of matured persons with Down syndrome remains 50 which remains widely variable **(Maltet al. 2013, Kavita Singh,** 2018b).

Prevalence

According to WHO estimates globally more than 450 million people suffer from mental disorders. Currently, mental and behavioral disorders account for 12% of the global burden of disease. This is likely to increase to15% by 2020. The major proportions of mental disorders come from low- and middle-income countries. The problem is further complicated by a lack of adequately trained manpower and a low priority of mental health in health policy (Reddy et al. 2013). In India, mental disorders have a prevalence of 1.05%. The urban population has a slightly higher rate being at 1.1% as compared to rural being at 1.008. Age was

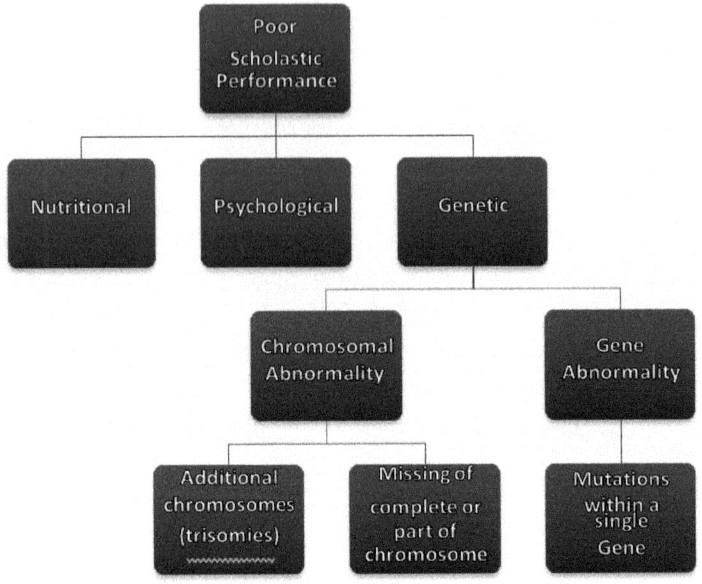

Causes of Poor Academic Performance

found to be highly correlated with the prevalence of children of rural areas (Lakhan et al.2015). The prevalence of mental retardation is influenced by a great number of environmental factors such as community age, racial and ethnic background, geographic region, and sex (Hernandez and Blazer, 2006). Social integration of a moderately mental retardate will be more difficult in a competitive, industrialized community than in a rural environment with the long-term support of an old-fashioned, extended family (Durkin et al. 1995).

The severely retarded are mostly identified before the age of one year, especially in the presence of physical abnormalities such as hydrocephaly, spasticity, and sensorial disturbances. Mildly mentally retarded individuals with IQs ranging between 50 and 70 are recognized at school. Once the critical period of adolescence and school attendance is over, however, many of the mildly mentally handicapped are assimilated into society and join the ranks of the dull-normal, living for the most part in marginal socio-economic circumstances. age (Boat and Wu, 2015). Almost all studies dealing with mental sub-normality in children report a higher incidence in males than in females. Moreover, in addition to the data collected from population and institution surveys, recent studies of family pedigrees more specifically demonstrate that X-linked recessive disorders represent a substantial proportion of mentally retarded males (Raymond, 2006).

Genetic Disorders

Genetic disorders are divided into two main groups. The first group includes chromosome disorders, such as Down syndrome, which may involve an entire chromosome including thousands of genes, while the second group involves only a single gene. Single gene disorders are divided into three main categories based on the mode of inheritance of the abnormal gene. The categories are autosomal recessive, autosomal dominant, and X-linked. Genes are found in pairs, as are chromosomes, and can have two or more alternative forms (alleles) occupying corresponding sites (loci) on homologous or partner chromosomes So for a given trait, the gene for that trait could be normal on both chromosomes of the pair, abnormal on both chromosomes of the pair or the gene could be normal on one chromosome and abnormal on the homologous or partner chromosome (Kavita Singh,2018b).

Autosomal Recessive Disorders

Autosomal recessive disorders occur when both genes or alleles at a given autosomal (autosome refers to chromosome numbers 1through 22 and excludes the sex chromosomes) sites are abnormal. Both genes on the pair of chromosomes must be abnormal for an individual to be affected by an autosomal recessive disorder. If one gene is abnormal and the other gene is normal for an autosomal recessive disorder, the individual will be unaffected by the disorder (M. E., Spitalnick, D. M., & Stark, J. A. 1992).

However, this individual will be a carrier of the defective form of the gene and could pass it on to his or her offspring. If both parents are carriers, one-fourth of their offspring are expected to be affected. Autosomal recessive disorders affect males and females with the same frequency and severity. The rarer the disorder the more likely the parents are related. Autosomal recessive disorders are often more severe, less variable, and less age-dependent than autosomal dominant disorders (McClearn, G. E. 1963)

Autosomal Dominant Disorders

Autosomal dominant disorders occur when either gene or allele on a pair of autosomal chromosomes is abnormal. If an individual is born with an abnormal form of a gene that causes autosomal dominant disorders, he or she will be affected and can also pass the defect to his or her offspring. The trait is inherited from one parent and one-half of the offspring are affected.

Isolated cases without a family history of the disorder may arise from new mutations with a 50% risk to their offspring. An autosomal dominant trait affects males and females with the same frequency and severity. Autosomal dominant disorders are often associated with malformations and are more variable but usually less severe than autosomal recessive disorders (Kavita Singh, 2018b).

X-Linked Disorders

X-linked disorders occur when the abnormal form of a gene is located on the X chromosome. There are two types of X-linked disorders, X-linked dominant and X-linked recessive. X-linked dominant conditions are rare and will not be discussed. X-linked recessive disorders are more common and of greater clinical significance particularly for families with the Fragile X syndrome.

In X-linked recessive disorders, males are most often affected. If a male has an X-linked recessive gene on his X chromosome, he has no normal X chromosome to compensate for the abnormal X-linked gene and he will be affected. He will pass the abnormal X chromosome to all of his daughters and he will pass his V chromosome to all of his sons. Therefore, if a male is affected with an X-linked recessive disorder then all of his daughters will be carriers and all of his sons will not have that particular X-linked trait. If a female has one normal X chromosome and one X chromosome containing an abnormal X- linked recessive gene, she will appear normal but will be an earner of the abnormal gene which may be passed on to her children The mother of an affected male is often a carrier and one-half of the sons of a carrier female are affected and one-half of her daughters are carriers (Thompson and Thompson, 1986; Kavita Singh,2018b).

• • •

CHAPTER III

CHROMOSOME IN MENTAL DISABILITY

Involvement of Chromosomes in Mental Disability

There are genetic components to mental disability. Examination of persons with chromosomal variations and mental disabilities may be a way of overcoming difficulties faced with the proper diagnostic processes Unfortunately, chromosomal analysis is rarely undertaken in subjects with psychiatric disorders. However, the rate of chromosomal abnormality has significantly increased in persons with learning disabilities, and maybe as high as 20% in those with a mild learning disability (Gostason et al. 1991). It has been established in many other medical conditions with a genetic basis that chromosomal variations, either by direct gene disorder or by positional effects, can produce identical or similar phenotypes to those caused by point mutations and their existence has greatly facilitated the physical mapping and cloning of candidate genes (Collins, 1992, 1995). Once a chromosomal anomaly is detected in a subject with a mental disability, it may be considered noncoincidental and related to the disorder if one or more of the following criteria are met: (a) the chromosomal abnormality is rare and there are independent reports of the abnormality being associated with mental disability; (b) there is the proximity of the abnormality with a region of suggestive linkage findings, or (c) there is cosegregation of the abnormality with mental disability within the patient's family (Evans et al. 2001)

Chromosome Structure

Chromosomal DNA is packaged in the nucleus with histone proteins (Fig.2). Histone proteins are positively-charged proteins that strongly hold on to negatively charged DNA strands and form complexes are known as nucleosomes. A nucleosome is made of DNA wound 1.65 times around 8 histone proteins. Nucleosomes fold over to form a 30-nanometer fiber called chromatin fiber that in turn forms loops being nearly 300 nanometers in length. A 250 nm wide fiber is then produced by compacting and folding of300 nm fibers which are tightly coiled into the chromatid of a chromosome(Annunziato, 2008)

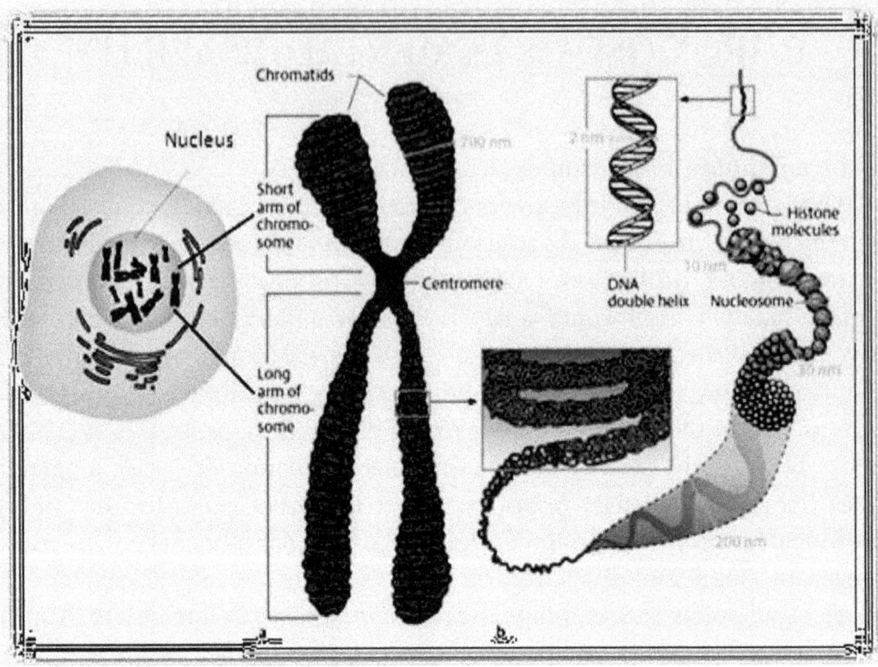

Fig. 2. Chromosome Structure exhibits DNA tightly-wound around histone

Human Chromosomes and Karyotype

Normal somatic cells of humans contain a diploid number of chromosomes (2n=46), or 23 pairs of chromosomes of which 22 pairs are autosomes with 1 pair of sex chromosomes being homologous XX in females and heterologous XY in males. The chromosomes derived from mother and fathers remain present in a diploid cell that contains equal genetic material, are comparable in morphology, and pair during meiotic cell division is known as homologous chromosomes. Sexual cells or gametes contain a haploid number of chromosomes (n=23). Union of two haploid gametes at fertilization produces diploid somatic cell aberrations (Mc Kusick, 1978). A karyotype is an exhibit of metaphase chromosomes of a diploid cell, detailing number, shape, size, and other markers like bands and satellites. This is a photomicrograph of the aligned chromosomes pairs that presents a visual demonstration of the chromosomal constitution of an organism. Karyotyping is the procedure of preparing a photomicrograph.

Chromosomes banding technique is used to identify the chromosome.

A metaphase chromosome consists of two sister chromatids which are connected by a centromere. There are two arms designated as „p" for a short one and „q" for a long arm, separated by the centromere. Telomeres at the tip of the chromatid possess a repetitive sequence of TTAGGG that protects the fusion of chromosomes and prevents DNA from exonucleases (O'Sullivan and Karlseder, 2010)

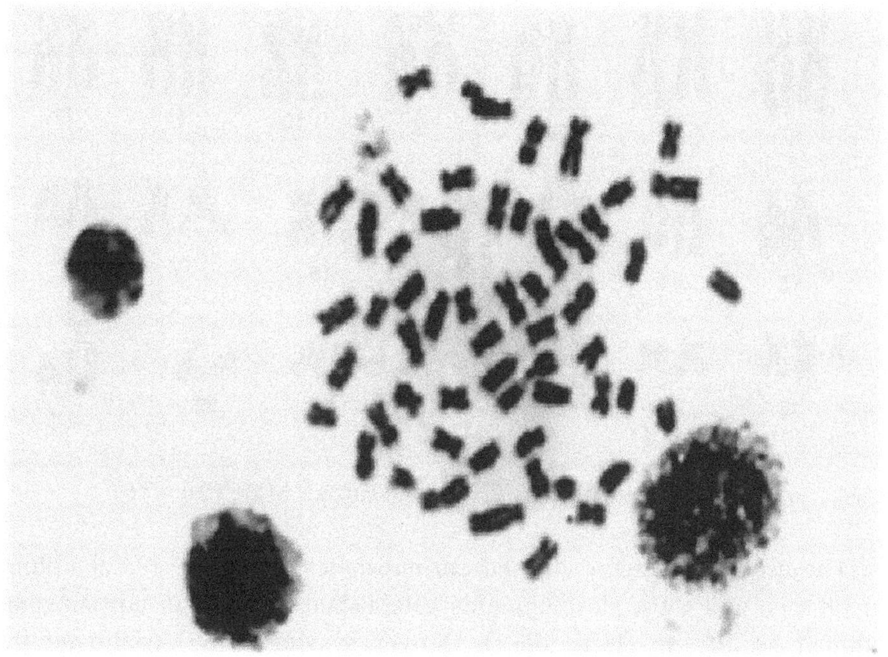

Fig 3. Chromosomes spread from a human cell before karyotyping

Earlier, human karyotype was made by simply staining chromosomes with Giemsa stain and squashing them with the coverslip and slide. The majority of cells were not at the appropriate mitotic phase and chromosome separation was undesirable and almost useless. The exact count of human chromosomes was also uncertain at that time and human chromosomes were considered to be 48 instead of 46. In 1952 a technician in the laboratory of T.C. Hsu accidentally substituted distilled water for the normal saline solution used in washing the cells just before squashing. This hypotonic treatment caused swelling of the cell nuclei and allowed the chromosomes to separate well.

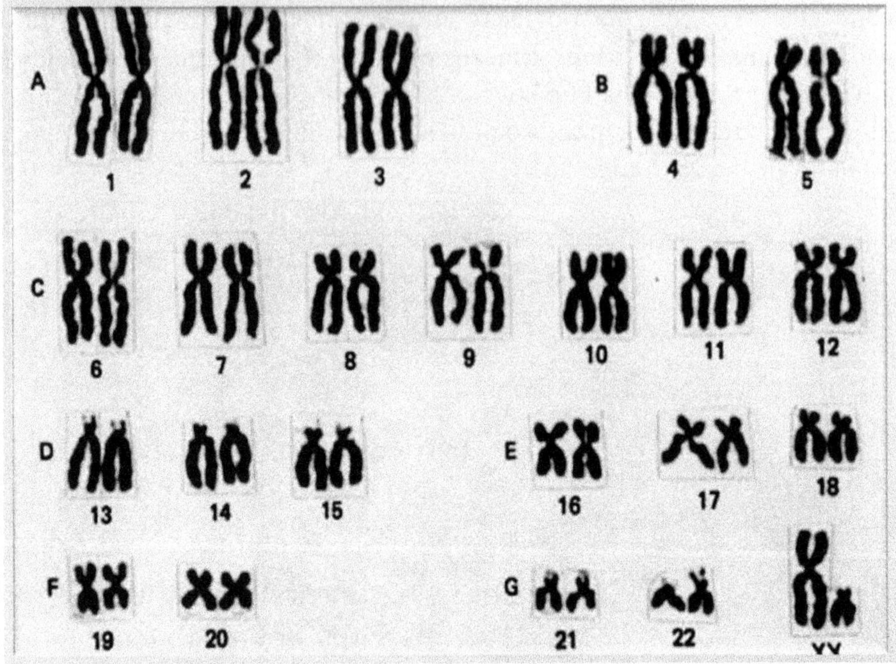

Fig 4. Karyotype of Normal Human Male (2n = 46)

The use of colchicine allowed chromosomes to be arrested at mitotic metaphase and these developments established the human chromosome number as 2n= 46 (Hsu, 1952). Denver System (1960) facilitated the classification of chromosomes into 7 groups (A to E) by their relative size and centromere position (Patau, 1960). Modern banding technoquesallowed each chromosome in the karyotype to be distinguished individually.

Chromosome Anomalies

Some variations in chromosomes are very small and they only involve a single gene called single-gene disorders. However, when variations in chromosomes are large enough and can be seen under a light microscope, they are called chromosome anomalies or aberrations. There are many types of chromosome anomalies (Kavita Singh, 2018b).

Chromosome anomalies usually occur when there is an error in cell division following meiosis or mitosis. They can be organized into two basic groups viz. Numerical anomalies (aneuploidy or an abnormal number of chromosomes) and Structural anomalies. Numerical anomalies occur due to nondisjunction where abnormal numbers of chromosomes may find their way into gametes, and a disorder of chromosome numbers may result(Hyman, S.L.2007). Alteration in chromosome structure can take several forms described as under:

- **Deletions:** A portion of the chromosome is missing or deleted.
- **Duplications**: A portion of the chromosome is duplicated
- **Translocations**: A portion of one chromosome is transferred to another chromosome.

There are two main types of translocations:

Reciprocal translocation: Segments from two different chromosomes have been exchanged.

Robertsonian translocation: An entire chromosome has attached to another at the centromere

- **Inversions:** A portion of the chromosome has broken off, turned upsidedown, and reattached, therefore the genetic material is inverted.

There are two main types of **Inversions**:

Paracentric inversions: Both breaks occur in one arm of the chromosome and do not include the centromere

Pericentric inversions: breaks occur in each arm of the chromosome and involved the centromere

- **Insertions:** A portion of one chromosome has been deleted from its normal place and inserted into another chromosome.
- **Rings:** A portion of a chromosome has broken off and formed a circle or ring. This can happen with or without the loss of genetic material.
- **Isochromosome:** Formed by the mirror image copy of a chromosome segment including the centromere.

The chromosomes observed at the metaphase stage possess two chromatids called sister chromatids. Chromatids of two different chromosomes are called non-sister chromatids (Reschly, D.J *et al*, 2002).

Conventionally, all the chromosomal aberrations are broadly divided into two groups.

Chromatid-type: In this type, breaks and re-joins always involve only one of the sister-chromatids at any one locus.

Chromosome-type: In this type, breaks and re-joins always involve both sister-chromatids at any one locus.

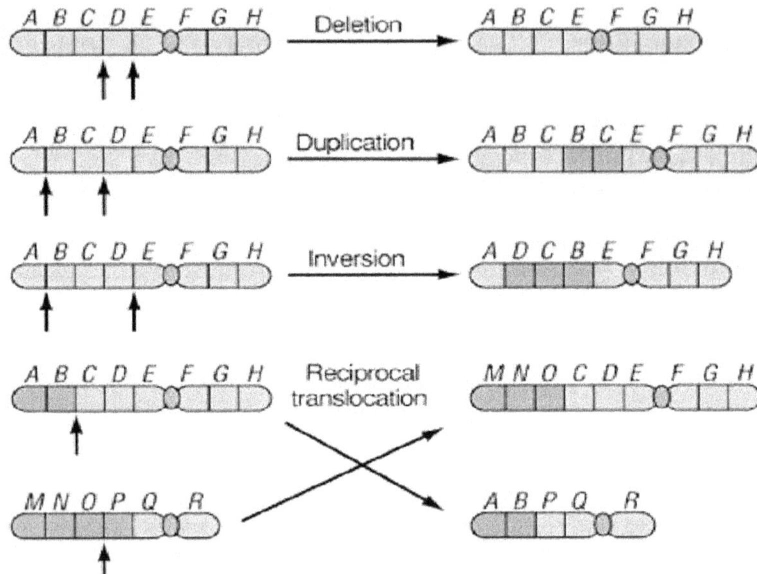

Source: Antonio, et al. "The Gale Encyclopedia of Science", edited by K.Lee Lerner and Brenda Wilmoth Lerner, 5th ed., Gale, 2014

Fig. 5 Several Forms of Alteration in Chromosome Structure

Sister Chromatid Exchange as a Marker of Genetic Variation

A coincidence of high chromosomal aberrations and Sister-chromatid exchanges has been reported frequently. Sister-chromatid exchange is a consequence of the interchange of replicating DNA between chromatids at apparently homologous loci. This is used as a method for determining the mechanism of chromosomal breakage and repair. Significant changes in the SCE are induced by mutagen or carcinogens, which provides the possibility of genetic change in cells (Carrano et al., 1978). Base-line SCE frequency is found variable due to several factors namely state of cells, condition of culture, or environmental factors.

Borgaonkar's Chromosomal Variation in Man Online Database

Chromosomal Variation in Man Online Database created by Borgaonkar supplies an incomparable means of consulting the literature on almost all common and uncommon chromosomal variations and abnormalities online. This has been systematized for trouble-free use; presentation is divided into three main subject areas involving variations and anomalies, numerical anomalies, and chromosomal breakage syndromes. The database reports details on the availability of mutant cell lines and demonstrates chromosome variations with a list that cross-references band numbers. Today, this Database has become an indispensable resource for cytogeneticists, human and medical geneticists, technicians working in the field of cytogenetics, and those who are interested in chromosome variations. (Borgaonkar, 1997, 2018)

General Incidence of Chromosomal Abnormalities

Chromosome variations account for the loss of an excessive proportion of all human conceptions. Nearly 15% of all predictable pregnancies terminate in spontaneous miscarriage and many more abnormal zygotes and embryos do not survive beyond the first few days or weeks of pregnancy (Turnpenny and Ellard, 2017). Given that nearly half of all spontaneous miscarriages have a chromosome abnormality. Presumably, the incidence of chromosome abnormalities at conception remains at least as high as 20% (Soler et al. 2017, Kavita Singh, 2018b). From conception onwards, the incidence of chromosome anomalies falls rapidly. By birth falls to a level of 0.5-1%, although the total is much higher if only stillborn infants are considered. It is notable that amongst the commonly recognized aneuploidy syndromes there is also an elevated proportion of spontaneous pregnancy loss. This has been confirmed by comparison of the incidence of conditions such as Down"s syndrome at the time of chorion villus sampling (10-11 weeks), amniocentesis (16 weeks), and birth (Alfirevic et al. 2003).

The development of a reliable technique for chromosome analysis in 1956 soon led to the discovery that several previously described conditions were due to an abnormality in chromosome number. Within three years the causes of Down"s syndrome (47, XY/XY,+21), Klinefelter"s syndrome (47, XXY), and Turner"s syndrome (45, X) had been established (Mc Kusick, 1978). Shortly afterward other autosomal trisomy syndromes were recognized and gradually over the ensuing years, many other multiple malformation syndromes were described in which there was loss or gain of chromosome material. (Kavita Singh, 2018b). Whilst on an individual base many of these are rare" together they make a major contribution to human morbidity and mortality. Chromosome abnormalities are now known to account for a large proportion of spontaneous pregnancy loss and childhood disability and can also contribute to the genesis of a significant proportion of malignancy in both childhood and adult life as a consequence of acquired somatic chromosome aberrations (Mc Kusick, 1978). The nomenclature system of human chromosomes and their arrangements were developed in a series of conferences beginning with the one organized by Dr. T. T. Puck in 1960 in Denver, Colorado, USA (Denver conference, 1960). The international system of Chromosome Nomenclature (ISCN) has facilitated communication and transmission of information in human cytogenetics (ISCN, 1985).

Common Chromosomal Anomalies in Mental Deficiency

Down syndrome: Down syndrome is unique in its prominent role in exploring the biology of mental retardation for the first time in 1866 by John Longdon Down whose contribution was significant in understanding the biology of normal and abnormal development (Down, 1866). The discovery of an extra 21 chromosome (trisomy 21) in the cells of individuals with Down syndrome exhibiting 47 chromosomes in place of 46 normal numbers by Professor Lejeune in 1959 established the role of chromosome variations in development (Kavita Singh, 2018b). This was the discovery of chromosome aneuploidy in man that firmly established the study of chromosomes called cytogenetic as a bona fide medical discipline (Smith and Warren, 1985; Patterson, 2009). Karyotype of normal human exhibits that chromosome 21 is one of the smallest autosomes, comprising nearly 1.9% of human DNA, Non-disjunction of this autosome during the formation of the gametes at meiosis I or meiosis II in one of the parents result in Down syndrome. Down syndrome is the most common genetic form of mental retardation followed by X-linked mental retardation (Kavita Singh, 2018b).

Fragile X syndrome: Fragile X syndrome (FXS) causes learning disabilities and cognitive impairment. Usually, the penetrance of this genetic condition is higher in males as compared to females because males are hemizygous having a single X-chromosome (McKusick, 1983). The maximum number of single genes that cause mental retardation are located on the X chromosome. The first identified gene was *FMR1* which causes fragile X syndrome is the commonest single gene abnormality. Fragile sites are heritable points on a chromosome that are susceptible to breakage and are consistently found on certain human chromosomes (Sutherland, 1982a, 1982b). These sites may represent structural chromosome mutations.

Syndrome Name	Prevalence	Chromosomal Abnormality	Sub localization to Chromosome Band
Down	1:650	Trisomy 21	21q22
Edwards	1:7,000	Trisomy 18	
Patau	1:12,000	Trisomy 13	
Trisomy 8#	1:25,000	Trisomy 8	
Wolf—Hirschhorn	1:50,000	Deletion of 4p	4p16
Cri-du-chat	1:50,000	Deletion of 5p	5p15
Sex chromosome abnormalit ies* of X and Y	Common	Deletion/duplication	
Martin—Bell (Fragile X)	1:1,200	Fragile site on Xq	Xq27
Dup (9p)	Rare	Duplication of 9p	
WAGR	Rare	Deletion of llp	11p13
Del (13q) with Retinoblastoma	Rare	Deletion of 13q	13q14 —>qter
Smith—Magenis	Rare	Deletion of 17p	17p11
Del (18p)	Rare	Deletion of 18p	
de Grouchy	Rare	Deletion of 18q	

Table 4. List of selective examples of Syndromes with Mental Retardation associated with Cytogenetically visible Chromosomal Abnormalities

*Adapted from a review of Raynham et al. (1996) based on the data summarized in Gorlin et al. (1990) *Although present in some cases, mental retardation is not consistently associated with sex chromosome abnormalities. # Affected subjects are usually mosaics for this abnormality.*

The fragile site on the long arm of the X (Xq 27.3) is associated with a form of familial X-linked mental retardation (Lubs, 1969). It has been estimated that from one-third to one-half of all families with (nonspecific) X-linked mental retardation express the fragile site in some proportion of their cells (Brookwell et al, 1982). The fragile site can be detected in chromosome preparations from lymphocytes grown in tissue culture media lacking folic acid and thymidine. Specific culture conditions can significantly alter the frequency with which the fragile site is expressed. Female carriers of this disorder may or may not express the fragile Xj some express it in only a small number of their cells. Thus, Xq fragile site demonstration in such carriers and in some affected males may be difficult due to a low level of expression. As with most X-linked recessive disorders, carrier detection is an important: aspect of genetic counseling for families with this syndrome. Males with Fragile X syndrome show mild to moderate intellectual disability whereas considerable proportions of females with this disorder being nearly one-third remain intellectually disabled. The majority of males and nearly half the females with fragile X syndrome show characteristic morphological features involving the long and narrow faces, prominent jaw and forehead, flat feet, large ears, and in males additionally enlarged testicles after puberty.

Disorder	Candidate Gene
ATR-X syndrome	XH2
CATCH-22 syndrome	TUPLE 1
Cockayne syndrome	ERCC6
Congenital myotonic dystrophy	Myotonin protein kinase
Duchenne muscular dystropy	Dystrophin
Fragile X syndrome	FMR-1
Menke's disease	MNK; ATP7A
Metabolic disorders	Many cloned genes
Milller—Dieker	LIS-1
Neurofibromatosis	N F-1
Norrie disease	NDP
Pel izaeus-Merzbacher	Proteolipid protein
Prader—Willi	SNRPN
Rubenstein-Taybi syndrome	CREB binding protein
Tuberous sclerosis	Tuberin
Wolf—Hirschhorn syndrome	ZNF141
X-linked hydrocephalus	LI CAM

Source - Review of Raynham et al. (1996)

Table 5. Disorders associated with MR for which candidate or causative genes have been identified

A mutation of FMR-1 known as fragile-X mental retardation gene located on the X- chromosome causes this syndromic condition. The FMR1 gene codes a protein known as fragile X mental retardation protein (FMRP) required for normal brain development. Incidence was noted in all races and ethnic groups. Nearly 10% of affected males have severe intellectual disability (Hagerman and Hagerman, 2002).

In Fragile X syndrome, the CGG pattern in a part of DNA in the FMR1 gene is repeated many times. In the majority of persons, the number of repeats remains small at 5 to 44 repeats, which is common whereas; when the number of repeats is very high being greater than 200 repeats, the gene turns off and protein production is halted leading to the development of FXS which is also known as trinucleotide repeat disorder. This is a heritable condition transmitted from parents. The intermediate number of repeats at nearly 45 to 54 may have a somewhat higher probability of having some symptoms but they do not have Fragile X syndrome (Willemsen et al. 2011). Sequence repeats in the range of 55-200 do not develop FXS but there may be the development of other conditions known as fragile X-associated disorder. Couples with premutation can transmit this to their children with the same condition or full mutation leading to the development of FXS (Gallagher and Hallahan, 2012).

The global prevalence of fragile X syndrome (FXS) in males is estimated at nearly 1 in 4,000 while in females it is nearly 1 in 5,000. It has been demonstrated in both animal and human studies that changes in the environment radically impact behavior (Restivo et al. 2005, Kavita Singh,2018b). A peaceful high-quality home environment has been found associated with fewer autistic behaviors, higher IQ scores, and better adaptability in children with Fragile X syndrome (Glaser et al. 2003).

• • •

CHAPTER IV

ETIOLOGICAL RESEARCH IN INTELLECTUAL DISABILITIES

In 1938 L.S. Penrose published "A clinical and genetic study of 1280 cases of mental defect" from the Royal Eastern Counties Institution, Colchester, England (Penrose, 1938; Kavita Singh, 2018b). In the preface, it is stated there can be no doubt that Dr. Penrose's methods, data, and results will to a large extent determine the general course of research in mental deficiency in this country for some years to come". An increase in the medical interest in the mentally retarded has been noted since the early sixties and was mainly stimulated by a progressively better understanding of biological mechanisms, involved in the causation of mental retardation. Several factors have stimulated this increased interest in research in mental retardation.

1. The discovery that a chromosomal anomaly, trisomy 21, was the cause of Down syndrome led to the description of other syndromes related to specific chromosomal abnormalities Except for a small number of sex-chromosome anomalies, these other entities were mostly discovered during studies of the mentally retarded. With the introduction of different chromosome banding techniques in 1970, the number of constitutional chromosomal syndromes increased to more than 120. More recently, prometaphase chromosome studies have revealed small chromosomal alterations in a number of previously delineated clinical syndromes involving Prader-Willi syndrome (15q proximal deletion) and tricho-rhino-phalangeal syndrome {8q deletion) (Down, 1866).

2. In the same period genetic counseling services were progressively established in university hospitals of industrialized countries. Individuals, couples, and families confronted with the occurrence of mental retardation from the beginning have been the largest and the most difficult group attending counseling clinics). Further research in the etiology of mental retardation, therefore, became necessary, as the quality of genetic counseling is directly dependent on the accuracy of etiological diagnosis. (Zhu, 2011)

3. Despite the explanation of X-linked mental retardation, there was no agreement on whether X-linked forms of mental retardation really existed or not until the early 70s. During several decades the surplus of male

mentally retarded patients had been attributed to errors in ascertainment such as the higher goals of expectation set for males in society, and for the alleged higher susceptibility of males to environmental hazards, such as birth trauma, hypoxia, immunization or infections. It is only after the description of the fragile Xq27-28 site by Lubs (1969) and the report of the relationship of this fragile X site and mental retardation, and its folic acid-dependent expression by Sutherland (1962a,b) that the existence of X-linked mental retardation was fully established. Since then, familial mental retardation, previously classified as being of psycho-social origin, has become a new field of intensive research. It was confirmed that X-linked mental retardation occurred in an important number of these families. In addition, it was shown that other genetic conditions, X-linked as well as autosomal, could be found in these families and identified as causative factors (Kavita Singh, 2018b)

4. An increasing number of mental disability-multiple malformation syndromes are currently being delineated by careful clinical observations off children and adults with malformative stigmata. The new research and developments in mental disability did not evolve at once. Some filtered through gradually and slowly following the growing evidence; others were born more quickly with the support of laboratory tests. Therapy as a more immediately attainable goal, the knowledge is used to inform individuals, couples and families about the nature of the disorder and the possibilities of prevention of genetically determined mental disability leading to poor academic performance in children, a major task for a genetic centre in the combat against the human suffering by genetic disease (KavitaSingh, 2018b).

Therapeutic Services

Various remedial services can improve adaptive behavioral skills in people with intellectual disabilities (ID, formerly mental retardation) but mere medical diagnosis is not sufficient for management of persons with intellectual disabilities. Parents need to do what is best for the child, and this can be best accomplished by Counseling and helping the parents learn how to live with this problem, plan for the child's future and help him achieve his maximum potential (Tarjan, 1965). Counseling is an integral part of the global efforts to manage people with intellectual disabilities. Counseling in intellectual disabilities has become a central and important element in a holistic model of health care. In this model, psychological issues are recognized as integral to client management. Counseling is a learning oriented process, carried on in a simple, one-to-one social environment, in which the counselor, professionally competent in relevant psychological skills and knowledge, seeks to assist the client, by methods appropriate to the latter"s needs and within the context of the total personnel program, to learn how to put such understanding into effect in relation to more clearly perceived, realistically defined goals to the end that the client may become a happier and more productive member of society (Kavita Singh, 2018b). Counseling is linked with bringing about an intentional change in the client. The counselor provides facilities to help achieve the desired change. The client alone is conscientious for the decisions or the choices he prefers, though the counselor may assist in this process by his tenderness and understanding relationship (Valente, 1972). Studies have revealed varied outcomes with regards to the efficacy of counseling to achieve either primary or secondary prevention goals. Abraham and Silva (2014) carried out a study that has proved that counseling is an effective tool for enhancing the QOL of subjects with HIV/AIDS. In this study, most of the subjects had psychological disorder. Counseling significantly revealed a positive change in the QOL of these subjects. Someday it may be possible to use genetic manipulations. This area of research attempts to correct the genetic causes of some IDs. However, this promising area of research is still in its infancy (Simmons, 2008).

• • •

CHAPTER V

MODUS OPERANDI

REQUIREMENTS

- **Consumable Items**

This category of general items used for the present study included different plastic wares, glassware, chemicals, other miscellaneous items, and equipment. The plastic wares used for the present study were supplied by Laxbro, Pune, India. Disposable syringes and needles for withdrawing fluid from vials and for dispensing cells were obtained from Hindustan Syringes and Medical Devices Ltd.India. Micropipettes and micro tips of different capacities were used in the present study and supplied by Fine Care Biosystems, Gujarat, India. The glassware used for the present study involved pipettes, culture flasks, glass bottles, ampoules for freezing, test tubes, centrifuge tubes, glass slides, containers, and filtration assembly of different capacities. Glasswares were mostly obtained from Borosil, Mumbai, India. There were various miscellaneous items used for the experimental work including surgical gloves, paper towels, etc.

Analytical grade chemicals including basic medium (RPMI 1640), antibiotics, buffering agents, growth supplements, colchicine, trypsin, etc. used for the present study were supplied by different chemical companies that involved Bengal Chemicals, Kolkata, India; Qualigens, Mumbai, India and Gibco, USA.

- **Equipment**

Many essential and useful additional equipment were used for the present study. A list of the main equipment used in the present study is provided in Table 6.

S.No.	Name of the Equipment	Make
1	Laminar air flow	Klenzoids, Mumbai, India
2	Centrifuge	Remi Equipments, Mumbai, India
3	Cyclomixer	Remi Equipment's, Mumbai
4	Hot air oven	Tempo Instruments & Equipment's Pvt. Ltd., Mumbai, India
5	Autoclave	Scientech, Delhi
6	Weighing balance	Sartorius, Mumbai, India
7	pH Meter	Jyoti Scientific Instruments, Gwalior, India
8	Vacuum pump	Acmevac Equipments, Mumbai, India
9	Slide warming plate	Scientech, Delhi, India
10	Magnetic stirrer	Scientech, Delhi, India

Table 6: Major Equipment

- **Subjects**

This cytogenetic study was carried out with the selective sampling of a total of 122 subjects of the age group of 6 to 18 years, comprised of 56 persons (34 male and 22 female) who had mental sublevels hence exhibited poor academic performance and 52 persons (32 male and 20 females) who were normal, taken as a control in the present study. The target group was chosen selectively from two hospitals where the hospital population involved schoolgoing children and schools as per the selection criteria. The control group was matched by age and sex.

- **Study Area**

Bhopal is the administrative centre of Madhya Pradesh state. Bhopal is also called the City of Lakes as there exist two fine-looking lakes involving the upper lake and lower lake collectively called the Bhoj Wetland. Bhopal city is one of the greenest cities in India. Bhopal (23°15 N; 77°25 E) is located in the central part of India, positioned in the north of the upper limit of the Vindhya mountain ranges. Bhopal has an average altitude of 427 meters (1401 ft). There are uneven elevations and small hills within the boundaries of Bhopal. It covers nearly 285.88 sq. km geographical area. As per the 2011 census, the population of Bhopal city is 1,798,218 involving 936,169 males and 862,049 females. It is forecasted to increase in 2018 to nearly 3.39 Million. The children (0-6 yr) population in this city was 226,931 in 2011. The population density of Bhopal is reported to be 855 persons/km2 (Census of India,2011). The rural population of the district is nearly 19.15 percent. The slum population of Bhopalis was reported to be 26.68 percent. The literacy rate on average remains at 83.47 percent (Census of India, 2011).

- **Methods**

The protocols of **Sharma and Sharma (1980)** for chromosome preparation was followed with slight variations in the present study:

Aseptic Technique

Despite the introduction of antibiotics, contamination by a microorganism or noxious chemical substances remains a major problem in tissue culture. For this reason, particular care has been taken in the selection and preparation of materials.

1. **Culture Room Fumigation**

The culture room was fumigated regularly at least once a month with 3% KMnO4 in1:1 N-Butanol: Formic Acid and kept closed overnight. The sterility of the culture room was monitored by exposing agar plates at regular intervals. The agar nutrient medium used for this purpose contained 3.0 gm Beef extract, 10.0 gm Peptone, 5.0 gm NaCl, 15.0 gm Agar dissolved in 1 liter of Double Distilled Water. The cultures were performed in the laminar airflow chamber. The surfaces of the areas of the laboratory used for culture work were cleaned both before and after use with 70% ethanol.

2. **Washing**

A very dilute solution of soap powder in water was prepared for soaking all the glassware and other selective assets immediately after use overnight. Care was taken that all the glassware are completely dipped in the soap solution. Glassware was scrubbed thoroughly by a bottle brush and rubber bungs from inside and outside. They were rinsed at least 3 times and left in running tap water for 4 to 5 hours. The washing was changed into distilled water and left overnight. Three changes of distilled water were given and dried in oven at a temperature of 60°C.

3. **Packing and Sterilization**

The caps of culture bottles were replaced. Syringes were wrapped in brown paper and needles were put in glass tubes with padding of cotton. For other glassware, the mouth was plugged with gauge and cotton foil. For the Pasteur pipette, the wider end was plugged with cotton and the fine end was sealed by flaming. All the glassware was packed in aluminium containers with lids (Tins). These were then sterilized in dry heat at a temperature of 120°C- 100°C for one hour. All the tins were stored in a dust-free place in the culture room.

Rubber bungs, liners, etc. were individually wrapped in aluminium foil and packed in aluminium tins before placing in autoclave drums. A piece of autoclave tape was put on the drums. Stuff was autoclaved under a pressure of 15 lb. for 15 minutes. When the color of the autoclaved tape changed to black, autoclaved stuff was transferred in an oven at a temperature of 60°C for drying of moisture.

Preparation of Tissue Culture Medium

The medium was prepared in the culture room using all aseptic precautions. RPMI 1640 culture media was used for the present study. 16.30 gm of RPMI 1640 powder was dissolved in 900 ml of autoclaved triple distilled water. 1 ml. of streptomycin (5000 IU/ml) and penicillin (5000 μg/ml) prepared in 0.85% saline and 0.29 gm L-glutamine was added followed by the addition of enough sodium bicarbonate to adjust the pH of the medium. For sterilization, the medium was passed through filtration assembly, using a membrane filter of the pore size of 0.22 μm. For rapid filtration, the assembly was connected to a suction pump working with negative pressure. Filtered media was divided equally into sterilized labeled bottles and stored at 4°C. For use in micro-cultures, media was mixed with 10% of fetal calf serum and 40 μg/ml of Phytohaemagglutinin (PHA-M).

The medium was filtered and distributed (5 ml each) to the culture vials and stored in a deep freeze at -20°C. The medium was thawed just before use. Once thawed, the medium was not refrozen. A sterility test of the medium was done by incubating small aliquots from the prepared medium for 24 hrs at 37°C. The medium was checked for microbial contamination after incubation.

Preparation of Reagents

1. Fixative: Carnoy's fixative was prepared for the fixation of the cultured lymphocytes by mixing one part of glacial acetic acid and three parts of methanol.
2. Hypotonic solution: 0.075 M KCl was used as a hypotonic solution for the lymphocytes. It was prepared by dissolving 0.57gm of KCl in a final volume of 100ml of double-distilled water.
3. Buffers: Buffer solutions were prepared by dissolving 1.42gm of disodium hydrogen phosphate anhydrous (Na2HP04) in 100ml of double distilled water and 1.56gm sodium dihydrogen phosphate monohydrate (NaH2P()4.H20) in 100ml of double distilled water separately.
4. Normal saline: Normal saline was prepared by dissolving 0.90gm of sodium chloride in 100ml of double-distilled water.
5. Trypsin solution: Trypsin solution was prepared by dissolving 20 mg of trypsin powder in 50ml of normal saline solution.

Preparation of Giemsa Stain

1. Giemsa stain (stock solution): Giemsa stock solution was prepared by addition of 1 gm of Giemsa powder to 50 ml of glycerol and 50 ml of methanol was added followed by overnight incubation at 60°C and the solution was stirred at room temperature over a magnetic stirrer. Then stain was filtered and stored at 4°C in an amber-coloured glass bottle.
2. Giemsa stain (working solution): For preparing a working solution, 6 ml of Giemsa stock solution was added to 40 ml of double-distilled water followed by the addition of 2 ml each of Na2HP04 and NaH2PO4 buffer solutions.

Chromosome Preparations

Cytologically, DNA can be studied at the chromosome level. Chromosomal analysis requires several cells in the division since it is only the metaphase stage that allows detailed study under the microscope. In humans, peripheral blood leucocytes offer one of the most feasible approaches to studying chromosomes. Circulating cells in the blood are at the resting stage. For in vitro culture resting leucocytes need stimulation to divide. Dividing cells are harvested to obtain mitotic figures/plates.

1. Peripheral Blood Sample Collection: 2 ml of peripheral blood was drawn in a heparinized disposable plastic syringe from each subject after taking informed consent of the subject. Setting up of a culture Heparinized peripheral venous blood samples were transferred into a sterile culture bottle under aseptic condition (in Laminar flow) and kept at 37°C for one hour and plasma was separated with a sterile syringe with a long 18 gauge needle. The bottle was kept tapping gently to get the settled white blood cells into suspension. The cells were transferred into a culture bottle containing 5 ml RPMI-1640 medium that was supplemented with L-glutamine, antibiotics, fetal calf serum, and Phytohaemagglutinin in the concentrations as described elsewhere in this chapter. The cultures were incubated in a CO2 incubator for 48 hours for the study of chromosome aberrations and 72 hr for SCEs.
2. Harvesting: 2 hr before the termination of the culture, colchicine (40 µg/ml) was added to each culture. After incubation, the cell suspensions were transferred into labeled centrifuge tubes and centrifuged for 10 minutes at 1000 rpm into pallets, and treated successively in hypotonic solution for 25 to30 min at 37°C. The cells were centrifuged and resuspended in fixative three times.
3. Preparation of slides: Slides were cleaned in alcohol or chromic acid and washed in running tap water before use. Two to three drops of cell suspension were dropped from a height on a clean wet slide. Slides were dried and prepared by warming on flame with care. Slides were marked and stored in dry and dust-free boxes for further use.
4. Staining: Air-dried slides were stained in Giemsa working solution for 5-8 minutes following the standard procedure with slight modifications as required (Goto et al. 1975; Moorhead et al. 1960)and the extra stain was removed by thoroughly rinsing the slides in tap water and finally in distilled water. Slides were ready to be screened directly.

G-Banding Technique

G-banding (Giemsa) is revealed by Giemsa staining of chromosome preparation after proteolytic enzyme treatment. It represents A-T rich regions. G-banding allows the characterization of individual chromosomes and their variants. G-banding of metaphases was done by treating them with trypsin solution for 20-60 seconds and then immediately rinsing them with normal saline solution to remove the extra trypsin. The slides were then stained with Giemsa working solution as described elsewhere in this chapter.

Microscopy

The slides were screened under the X10 objective. Nearly one hundred well-spread metaphases were recorded per sample. Each metaphase was viewed again under the X100 oil immersion objective. Counting of chromosome numbers and microscopic analysis of individual chromosomes were done. Chromosomal aberrations were recorded in a standard format and classified according to the International Nomenclature (ISCN, 1995). Hansson (1970)suggested that the satellite ends of the associating chromosomes had to be directed towards each other with their longitudinal axes meeting between their short arms. Moreover, the distance between the centromeres of associated chromosomes should not exceed the total length of one 'G' chromosome after excluding its satellite.

Family Studies

Selective families were studied to record the history of the incidence of poor academic performance.

Statistical Analysis

General rules for forming percentile frequency distributions were followed. Relative and cumulative frequency distributions of various parameters were presented with standard error and standard deviation measurements and applied tests of significant difference. Useful statistical analysis for different categories/ groups of selective population and control was also done by applying standard procedures.

• • •

CHAPTER VI

STUDY OUTCOMES

Baseline Characteristics of the Sampled Population

This cytogenetic study was carried out with the selective sampling of a total of 122 subjects of the age group of 6 to 18 years, comprised of 56 persons (34 male and 22 female) who had mental sublevel hence exhibited poor academicperformance and 66 persons (39 male and 27 female) who were normal, taken as a control in the present study. There were 59.84% males and 40.16% females. The target group was chosen selectively from two hospitals where the hospital population involved school- going children and schools as per the selection criteria. The control group was matched by age and sex.

Characteristics	Frequency (n=122)		
Sex	All	Subjects with mental sublevel	Control
Male	73 (59.84%)	34	39
Female	49 (40.16%)	22	27
Total	122	56	66
Age (Years)			
6-10	27 (22.13%)	12	15
11-14	33 (27.05%)	17	16
15-18	62 (50.82%)	27	35
Total	122	56	66

Figures in parentheses are percentage of the total

Table 7: Socio-demographic characteristics of recruited children (Sex and Age)

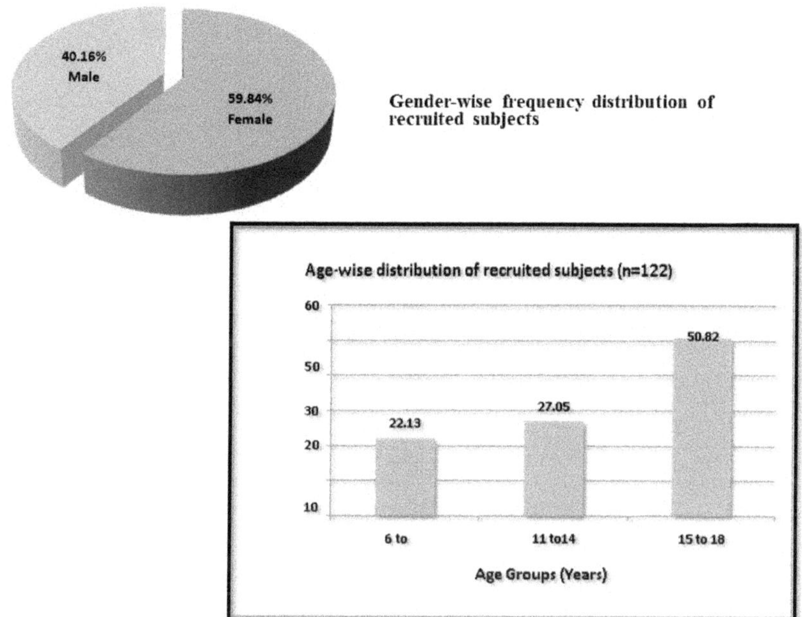

Fig. 6 Gender-wise and Age-wise frequency distribution of recruited subjects

There were 59.84% males and 40.16% females (Fig, 6). The majority of children being 50.82% belonged to the age group of 15 -18 years followed by 27.05% of children of the age group 11-14 years. Furthermore, 22.13% of children belonged to the age group 6-10 years (Table 7; Fig 6).

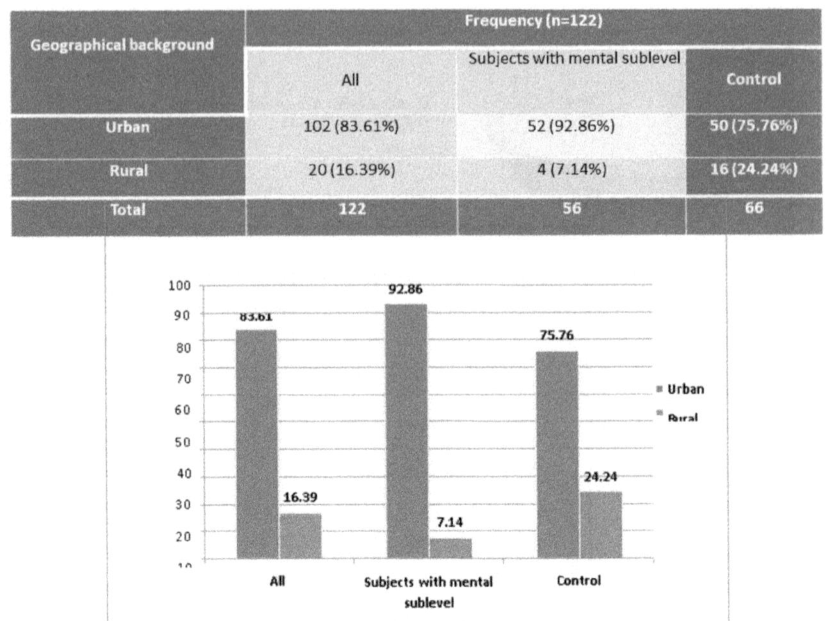

Geographical background	Frequency (n=122)		
	All	Subjects with mental sublevel	Control
Urban	102 (83.61%)	52 (92.86%)	50 (75.76%)
Rural	20 (16.39%)	4 (7.14%)	16 (24.24%)
Total	122	56	66

Table 8: Geographical background of recruited subjects

In both urban as well as rural settings. Children from urban areas were 83.61%and the rest 16.39% were from rural areas (Table 8). Of these, 92.86% of subjects with mental sub-level were from urban settings, and the rest 7.14% were from rural settings. On the other hand, 75.76% of normal subjects (control) were from urban settings, and the rest 24.24% were from rural settings .

Socio-Economic Status	Frequency (n=122)
Below Poverty line	30 (26.59%)
Lower-middle	26 (21.31%)
Middle	42 (34.43%)
Upper	24 (19.67%)
All	122

Table 9 Socio-Economic Status of Recruited Subjects

Samples were divided into four groups based on their socio-economic status. Majority of them were from middle class being at 34.43% followed by children belonging to Below Poverty line being at 26.59%. Furthermore, 21.31% children belonged to Lower-middle class children followed by Upper class children being at19.67% (Table 9)

Parameter	Male		Female	
	n	Mean ± S.D. (Range)	n	Mean + S.D. (Range)
Age (Years)	32	13.68 ± 4.8 (6-18)	22	11.87 ± 5.62 (6-17)
Weight (Kg)		39.86 ± 9.28 (17-59)		33.21 ± 8.51 (15-57)
Height (cm)		148.64 ± 14.40 (109-178)		143.45 ± 10.26 (113-154)

Anthropometric measures of children with mental sub-level

Parameter	Male		Female	
	n	Mean ± S.D. (Range)	n	Mean + S.D. (Range)
Age (Years)	39	14.22 ± 5.70 (6-18)	27	12.34 ± 5.52 (6-18)
Weight (Kg)		39.73 ± 7.96 (17-65)		33.66 + 6.44 (16-63)
Height (cm)		150.21 ± 10.93 (112-171)		155.17 ± 8.76 (103-177)

Anthropometric measures of normal children chosen as control

Table 10:Anthropometric Measures

Table 10 depicts selective anthropometric measures of children with mental sub-level. The mean age (years) of this group of children were 13.68 ± 4.8 and 11.87 ± 5.62 in male and female children respectively. The mean weight (Kg) was 39.86 ± 9.28 and 33.21 ± 8.51 in male and female children respectively. The mean height (cm) in male subjects was 148.64 ± 14.40 whereas, it was 143.45 ±10.26 in females. Table10 depicts selective anthropometric measures of normal children chosen as control. The mean age (years) of this group of children were 14.22 ± 5.70 and 12.34 ± 5.52 in male and female children respectively. The mean weight (Kg) was 39.73 ± 7.96 and 33.66 ± 6.44 in male and female children respectively. The mean height (cm) in male subjects was 150.21 ± 10.93 whereas, it was 155.17 ± 8.76 in females.

Intellectual disability in subjects with mental sub-level

There were variable levels of intellectual disability in selective subjects with mental sub-level. Out of a total of 56 children recruited from this group, a majority being 21 had moderate intellectual disability (IQ 36-51) followed by 16 with mild intellectual disability (IQ 52-69) status. Furthermore, 13 children showed severe Intellectual disability (IQ 20-35) and there were only 6 children who had profound intellectual disability (IQ 19 or below)

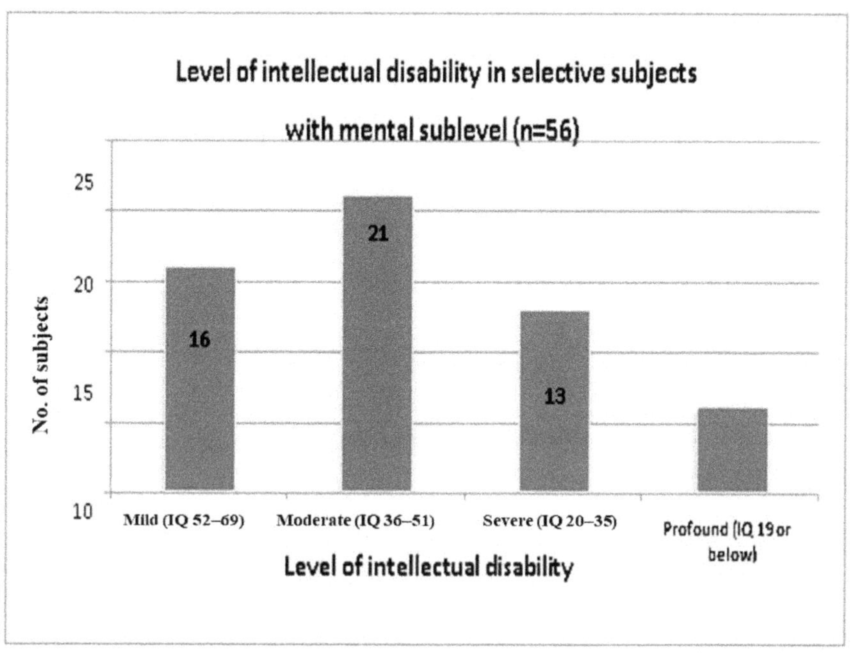

Fig,7: Intellectual disability

• • •

CHAPTER VII

CHROMOSOMAL ABNORMALITIE

Table 11 demonstrates frequency of chromosomal abnormalities in subjects with intellectual disability and control. In this study, significantly higher 44.64% subjects with intellectual disability showed varied chromosomal abnormalities as compared to Control group which showed 15.15%. Frequency was 29.49% higher in subjects with mental sub-level. In control group, 84.84% subjects showed normal karyotype being significantly higher as compared to subjects with mental sub-level which showed these to be 55.35%.

Group	Subjects			
	Chromosomal abnormalities		Normal Karyotype	
	n	%	n	%
Subjects with intellectual disability	25 (56)	44.64	31 (56)	55.35
Control	10 (66)	15.15	56 (66)	84.84

Frequency of Chromosomal abnormalities in subjects with intellectual disability and control

Figures in parentheses are total samples in the group

Group	Subjects with intellectual disability	Control
Subjects	56	66
No. of metaphases	1280	1350
Total aberrant metaphases (Mean ± S.E)	38.26 ± 2.62	12.15 ± 4.33*

Aberrant metaphases in subjects with intellectual disability and in control

*Statistically significant difference (p<0.01

Table 11:Chromosomal abnormalities

Table 12 show number of total metaphases screened and mean values of aberrant metaphases in subjects with intellectual disability and in control. A total of 1280 metaphases were screened in 56 samples belonging to subjects with mental sub-level. The mean value of the aberrant metaphases was 38.26 ± 2.62. On the other hand, 1350 metaphases were screened in 66 samples belonging to normal subjects taken as control in the present study. The mean value of the aberrant metaphases In control group was 12.15 ± 4.33 (Table 12) showing statistically significant difference (p<0.01).

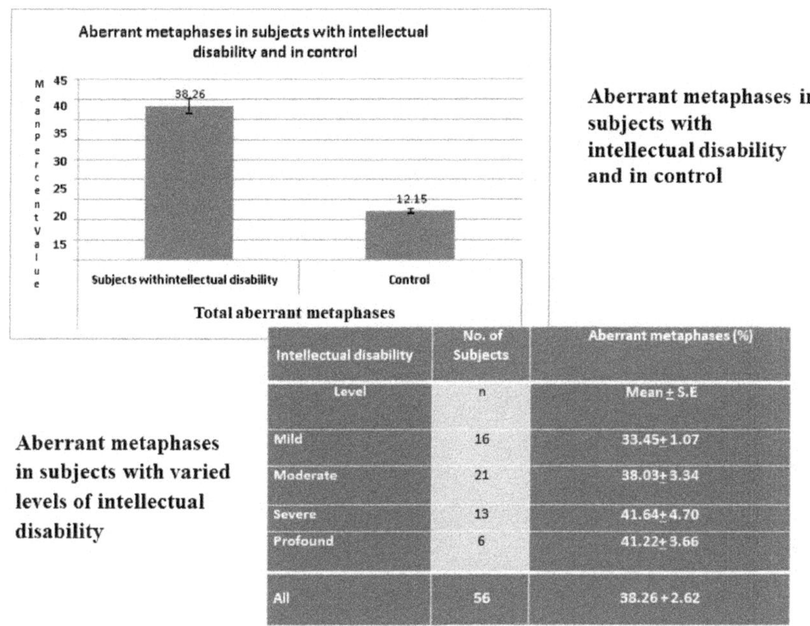

Aberrant metaphases in subjects with intellectual disability and in control

Aberrant metaphases in subjects with varied levels of intellectual disability

Intellectual disability	No. of Subjects	Aberrant metaphases (%)
Level	n	Mean ± S.E
Mild	16	33.45± 1.07
Moderate	21	38.03± 3.34
Severe	13	41.64± 4.70
Profound	6	41.22± 3.66
All	56	38.26 + 2.62

Table 12: Aberrant Metaphases

Table 12 depicts mean values of aberrant metaphases in subjects with varied levels of intellectual disability. A total of 6 subjects out of 56 had profound intellectual disability and showed mean value of aberrant metaphases at 41.22+ 3.66. Subjects having severe intellectual disability were 13 in the series and showed mean value at 41.64+ 4.70. Subjects with moderate intellectual disability were 21 in the series and showed mean value at 38.03 +3.34. There were 16 subjects who had only mild intellectual disability showing mean value at 33.45+ 1.07. Differences were not statistically significant. Overall mean value in 56 subjects worked out to be at 38.26 ± 2.62.

Table 13 depicts chromosomal abnormalities in subjects with intellectual disability. Out of 56 subjects who had intellectual disability, 25 exhibited varied chromosomal abnormalities. Gender-wise distribution in this revealed that 76% male subjects and 24% female subjects had chromosomal abnormalities. Both autosomal and sex chromosome abnormalities were observed. There were structural as well as numerical abnormalities of autosomes in the subjects investigated whereas, only structural abnormalities were found in the series of sex chromosome abnormalities. Majority of autosomal aberrations being 22 (88%) were structural in the series and only 1 (4%) showed numerical abnormality of autosome being trisomy of 21 chromosome in a male out of a total of 25 detected with different types of chromosome abnormalities (Fig .8). Structural sex chromosomal abnormalities were noted in 2 subjects comprising 1 male and 1 female. Normal karyotypes were also observed in 31 (55.35%) subjects who had intellectual disability.

Frequency (n=56)									
Chromosomal Abnormality	Structural			Numerical			Total		
	M	F	All	M	F	All	M	F	All
Autosomal abnormalities	17 (68)	5 (20)	22 (88)	1 (4)	0 (0)	1 (4)	18 (72)	5 (20)	23 (92)
Sex chromosomal abnormalities	1 (4)	1 (4)	2 (8)	0 (0)	0 (0)	0 (0)	1 (4)	1 (4)	2 (8)
Pooled	18 (72)	6 (24)	24 (96)	1 (4)	0 (0)	1 (4)	19 (76)	6 (24)	25 (100)
Normal Karyotype	-	-	-	-	-	-	15 (48)	16 (52)	31 (100)

Table 13: Chromosomal Abnormalities in subjects with Intellectual Disability

Table 14 depicts chromosomal abnormalities in normal subjects chosen as control. Out of 66 subjects who were normal and taken as control, 10 exhibited varied chromosomal abnormalities. Gender-wise distribution in this revealed that 60% male subjects and 40% female subjects had c hromosomal abnormalities. Both autosomal and sex chromosome abnormalities were observed in this set of samples as well. There were only structural abnormalities of autosomes and sex chromosome (Fig.8). Structural sex chromosomal abnormality was noted in only 1 female subject. Normal karyotypes were frequently observed in 56 (88.84%) subjects who were normal.

Chromosomal Abnormality	Frequency (n=66)								
	Structural			Numerical			Total		
	M	F	All	M	F	All	M	F	All
Autosomal abnormalities	6 (60)	3 (30)	9 (90)	0 (0)	0 (0)	0 (0)	6 (60)	3 (30)	9 (90)
Sex chromosomal abnormalities	0 (0)	1 (10)	1 (10)	0 (0)	0 (0)	0 (0)	0 (0)	1 (10)	1 (10)
Pooled	6 (60)	4 (40)	10 (100)	0 (0)	0 (0)	0 (0)	6 (60)	4 (40)	10 (100)
Normal Karyotype	-	-	-	-	-	-	33 (59)	23 (41)	56 (100)

Table 5.10. Chromosomal abnormalities in Normal Subjects chosen as Control

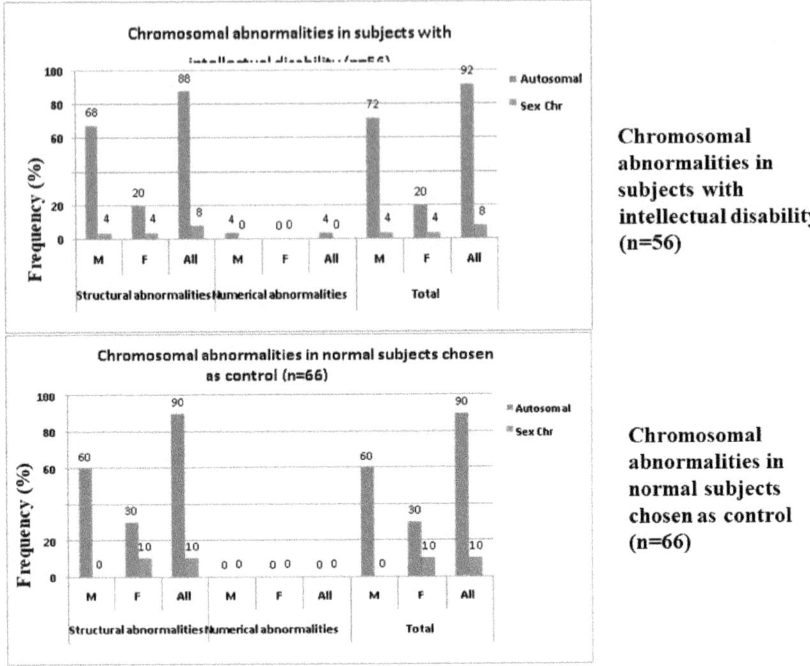

Chromosomal abnormalities in subjects with intellectual disability (n=56)

Chromosomal abnormalities in normal subjects chosen as control (n=66)

Fig. 8 : Chromosomal abnormalities with intellectual disability and Normal Subjects

• • •

CHAPTER VIII

CHROMOSOME TYPE AND CHROMATID TYPE

Table 15 presents chromosome type and chromatid-type aberrations in subjects with intellectual disability and in control. Chromatid-type aberrations were more frequent in both the groups involving subjects with intellectual disability and in control and observed to be 13 (52%) out of 25 and 6 (60%) out of 10 respectively. Chromosome-type aberrations were observed in 9 (36%) whereas, multiple-type aberrations were noted in 3 (12%) samples belonging to the subjects with intellectual disabilities. Chromosome-type aberrations were also observed in the control group, though in a low frequency, detected in 3 (30%) subjects, multiple- type aberrations were noted in only 1 (10%) samples.

Type	Subjects	
	Subjects with Intellectual Disability	Control
Chromosome-type*	9 (36.0)	3 (30.0)
Chromatid- type*	13 (52.0)	6 (60.0)
Multiple- type	3 (12.0)	1 (10.0)
All	25	10

Figures in parentheses are percentage of the total in the column
*Statistically significant difference ($p<0.05$).

Table 15. Chromosome type and chromatid- type aberrations in subjects with intellectual disability and in control

Table 16 depicts chromosome-type aberrations in subjects with intellectual disability and in control. In subjects with intellectual disability, ring chromosomes (RC) were observed in 4 subjects (44.4% in the series) whereas, Dicentric chromosomes (DC) were observed in 2 (22.2% in the series). Acrocentric associations (ACA) were also observed in 2 (22.2% in the series). There was only 1 sample (11.1% in the series) where Acentric fragments (ACF) were observed.

Type	Subjects			
	Subjects with intellectual disability		Control Group	
	n	%*	n^	%*
Ring chromosomes (RC)	4	44.4	1	25.0
Dicentric chromosomes (DC)	2	22.2	1	25.0
Acentric fragments (ACF)	1	11.1	-	-
Acrocentric associations (ACA)	2	22.2	2	50.0
All	9	100	4^	100

* Figures are percentage of the total in the column

^1 sample with multiple type aberrations involved chromosome-type abnormality

Table 16. Chromosome-type aberrations in subjects with Intellectual Disability and in Control

Frequencies of varied chromosome-type aberrations were lower in the control group comprised of normal children as compared to the group of subjects with intellectual disabilities. Ring chromosomes (RC) and Dicentric chromosomes (DC) were observed in separate single samples (25.0% each in the series) whereas, 2 samples (50% in the series) exhibited Acrocentric associations (ACA) of which 1 belonged to the sample that showed multiple aberrations involving chromosome-type abnormality.

Type	Subjects			
	Subjects with intellectual disability		Control Group	
	n^	%*	n	%*
Chromatid breaks (CB)	8	53.3	2	33.3
Gaps (G)	4	26.6	3	50.0
Terminal deletions (TD)	3	20.0	1	16.7
All	15^	100	6	100

* Figures are percentage of the total in the column
^2sample with multiple type aberrations involved chromatid-type abnormality

Table 17. Chromatid- type aberrations in subjects with Intellectual Disability and in Control

Table 17. depicts chromatid-type aberrations in subjects with intellectual disability and in control. In subjects with intellectual disability, Chromatid breaks (CB) were observed in 8 subjects (53.3% in the series) whereas, Gaps (G) was observed in 4 (26.6% in the series). Terminal deletions (TD) were observed in 3 subjects (20.0% in the series). In this series two samples with multiple-type aberrations involved chromatid-type abnormality

As noted in the case of chromosome-type aberrations, frequencies of varied chromatid-type aberrations were lower in the control group comprised of normal children as compared to the group of subjects with intellectual disabilities. In this series, Chromatid breaks (CB) were observed in 2 subjects (33.3% in the series) whereas, Gaps (G) were observed in 3 subjects (50.0% in the series). Terminal deletions (TD) were observed in the sample of a single subject.

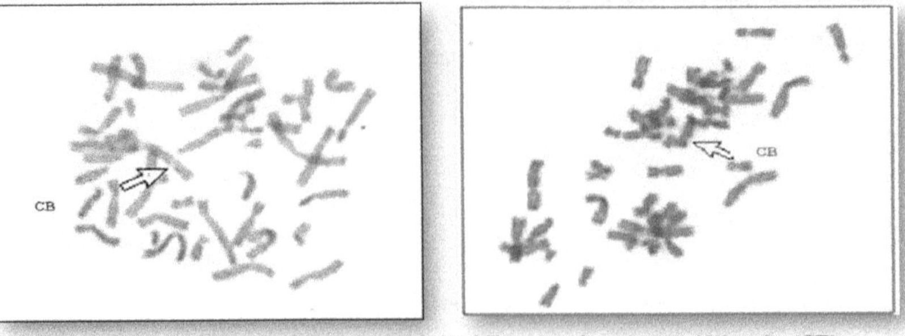

Metaphases of in subjects with intellectual disability showing chromatid breaks (CB).

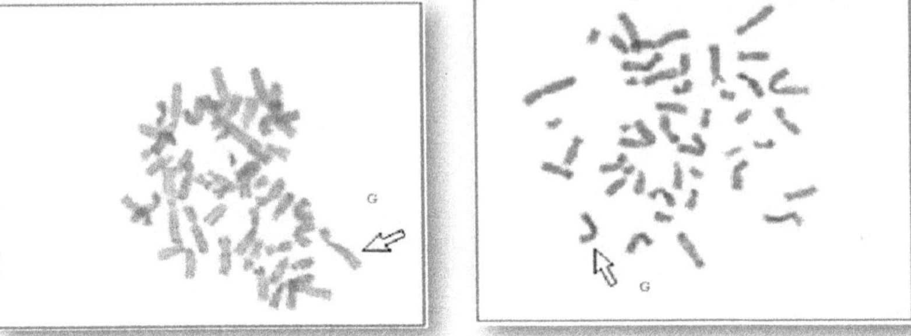

Metaphases of in subjects with intellectual disability showing gaps (G)

Fig. 9: Metaphases of Subjects

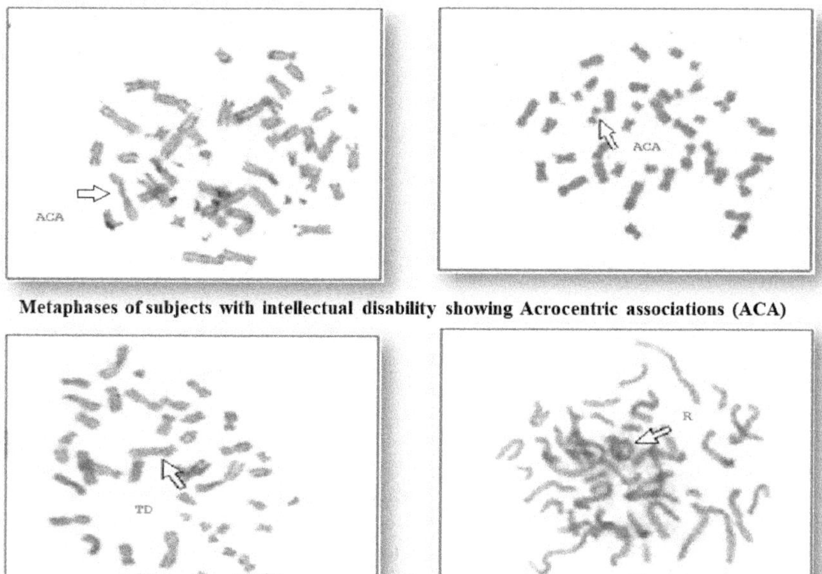

Metaphases of subjects with intellectual disability showing Acrocentric associations (ACA)

Metaphase of a subject with intellectual disability showing terminal deletion (TD)

Metaphase of a subject with intellectual disability showing ring chromosome (R)

Fig 10: Metaphase of Subjects showing ACA,TD,R

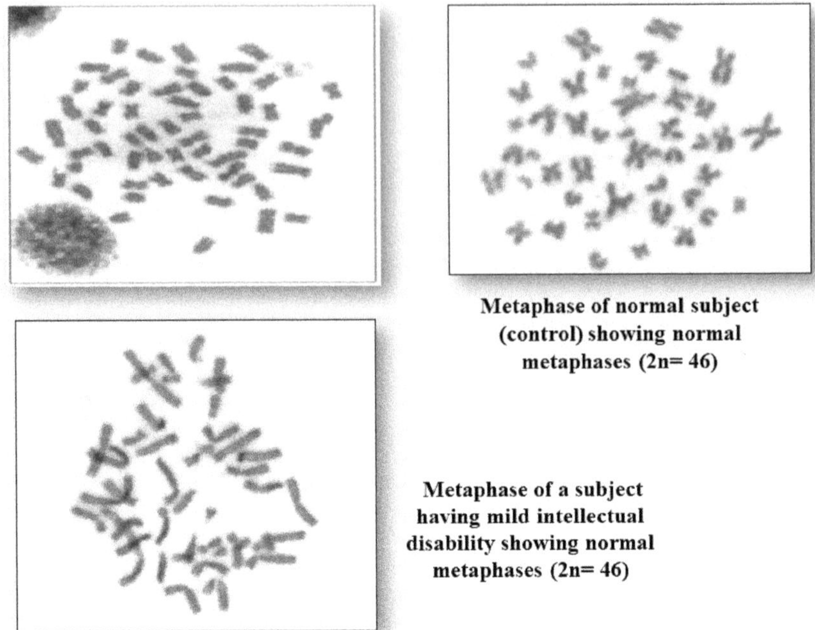

Metaphase of normal subject (control) showing normal metaphases (2n= 46)

Metaphase of a subject having mild intellectual disability showing normal metaphases (2n= 46)

Fig 11: Metaphase of a Subject showing Normal Metaphase

• • •

CHAPTER IX

DENOUEMENT

The present study focuses on cytogenetic anomalies in poor academic children of Bhopal and revealed the association of chromosomal aberrations with intellectual disability. Intellectual disability may result in poor academic performance among children before the age of 18 years. Poor academic performance is characterized by significant limitations in both intellectual functioning and adaptive behavior affecting significant proportions of the children population in India and in the world. The traits of an individual are products of the interaction of genetic makeup and environment. Interactions of genes and environment can result in different disease phenotypes and intellectual abilities (McKusick, 1983). There is a connection between DNA sequences and behavioral differences such as intelligence. DNA differences can lead to behavioral differences however; behavioral differences do not change DNA sequences (Deary et al. 2006; Lubs, 1969). The present study principally involved cytogenetic investigations carried out with the selective sampling of 122 subjects up to 18 years of their age, comprising both males and females who had Intellectual disabilities of varying levels and normal children taken as control (Kavita Singh, 2018a,b; 2019).

Selective anthropometric measures of children with mental sub-level were noted in the present study. The mean weight (Kg) was 39.86 ± 9.28 and 33.21 ± 8.51 in male and female children respectively. The mean height (cm) in male subjects was 148.64 ± 14.40 whereas; it was 143.45 ± 10.26 in females. In normal children chosen as control, the mean weight (Kg) was 39.73 ± 7.96 and 33.66 ± 6.44 in male and female children respectively. The mean height (cm) in male subjects was 150.21 ± 10.93 whereas; it was 155.17 ± 8.76 in females. This revealed slight insignificant differences in weight and height in both the groups with slightly higher values in normal children as compared to children with intellectual disabilities. Sucuoğlu, Esen, and Alkoç, Gülçiçek (2017) in their study carried out among children of a nursery school in Istanbul demonstrated that the head and neck circumference of children with an intellectual disability is thicker as compared to the head and neck circumference of normally developed children. Furthermore, the weights of normally developed children noted were higher as compared to the mentally deficient children.

It was observed in the present study that there were variable levels of intellectual disability in selective subjects with mental sub-level. Out of a total of 56 children recruited from this group, a majority being 21 had moderate intellectual disability (IQ 36-51) followed by 16 with mild intellectual disability (IQ 52-69) status. Furthermore, 13 children showed severe Intellectual disability (IQ 20-35) and there were only 6 children who had profound intellectual disability (IQ 19 or below). Nouwens (2017) demonstrated the identification of classes of persons with a mild intellectual disability or borderline intellectual functioning and examined whether these classes are related to individual and/or environmental characteristics.

The present research study demonstrated the frequency of chromosomal abnormalities in subjects with intellectual disability and control. Significantly higher 44.64% of subjects with intellectual disability showed varied chromosomal abnormalities as compared to the control group which showed 15.15%. Frequency was 29.49% higher in subjects with mental sub-level. In the control group, 84.84% of subjects showed normal karyotype being significantly higher as compared to subjects with mental sub-level which showed these to be 55.35%. The mean value of the aberrant metaphases in subjects with mental sub-level was 38.26 ± 2.62 whereas, it was considerably low being 12.15 ± 4.33 in normal control showing a statistically significant difference ($p<0.01$)

The present study depicted the mean values of aberrant metaphases in subjects with varying levels of intellectual disability. A total of 6 subjects out of 56 had a profound intellectual disability and showed a mean value of aberrant metaphases at 41.22+ 3.66. Subjects having a severe intellectual disability were 13 in the series and showed a mean value of 41.64+ 4.70. Subjects with moderate intellectual disability were 21 in the series and showed a mean value of 38.03+3.34. There were 16 subjects who had only mild intellectual disability showing a mean value of 33.45+ 1.07. Differences were not statistically significant. The overall mean value in 56 subjects worked out to be 38.26 + 2.62.

Out of 56 subjects who had intellectual disabilities, 25 exhibited varied chromosomal abnormalities. Gender-wise distribution in this revealed that 76% of male subjects and 24% of female subjects had chromosomal abnormalities. Both autosomal and sex chromosome abnormalities were observed. There were structural as well as numerical abnormalities of autosomes in the subjects investigated whereas, only structural abnormalities were found in the series of sex chromosome abnormalities. The majority of autosomal aberrations being 22 (88%) were structural in the series and only 1 (4%) showed numerical abnormality of autosomes being trisomy of 21 chromosomes in a male out of a total of 25 detected with different types of chromosome abnormalities.

Structural sex chromosomal abnormalities were noted in 2 subjects comprising 1 male and 1 female. Normal karyotypes were also observed in 31 (55.35%) subjects who had an intellectual disability. Out of 66 subjects who were normal and taken as control, 10 exhibited varied chromosomal abnormalities. Gender-wise distribution in this revealed that 60% of male subjects and 40% of female subjects had chromosomal abnormalities. Both autosomal and sex chromosome abnormalities were observed in this set of samples as well. There were only structural abnormalities of autosomes and sex chromosomes. Structural sex chromosomal abnormality was noted in only 1 female subject. Normal karyotypes were frequently observed in 56 (88.84%) subjects who were normal.

Chromatid-type aberrations were more frequent in both the groups involving subjects with intellectual disability and in control and observed to be 13 (52%) out of 25 and 6 (60%) out of 10 respectively. Chromosome-type aberrations were observed in 9 (36%) whereas, multiple-type aberrations were noted in 3 (12%) samples belonging to the subjects with intellectual disabilities. Chromosome-type aberrations were also observed in the control group, though in a low frequency, detected in 3 (30%) subjects, multiple-type aberrations were noted in only 1 (10%) samples. The present study depicted chromosome-type aberrations in subjects with intellectual disability and in control. In subjects with intellectual disability, ring chromosomes (RC) were observed in 4 subjects (44.4% in the series) whereas, Dicentric chromosomes (DC) were observed in 2 (22.2% in the series). Acrocentric associations (ACA) were also observed in 2 (22.2% in the series).

There was only 1 sample (11.1% in the series) where Acentric fragments (ACF) were observed. Frequencies of varied chromosome-type aberrations were lower in the control group comprised of normal children as compared to the group of subjects with intellectual disabilities. Ring chromosomes (RC) and Dicentric chromosomes (DC) were observed in separate single samples (25.0% each in the series) whereas, 2 samples (50% in the series) exhibited Acrocentric associations (ACA) of which 1 belonged to the sample that showed multiple aberrations involving chromosome-type abnormality. Furthermore, the study depicted chromatid-type aberrations in subjects with intellectual disability and in control. In subjects with intellectual disability, Chromatid breaks (CB) were observed in 8 subjects (53.3% in the series) whereas, Gaps (G) was observed in 4 (26.6% in the series). Terminal deletions (TD) were observed in 3 subjects (20.0% in the series). In this series two samples with multiple-type aberrations involved chromatid-type abnormality. As noted in the case of chromosome-type aberrations, frequencies of varied chromatid-type aberrations were lower in the control group comprised of normal children as compared to the group of subjects with intellectual disabilities. In this series, Chromatid breaks (CB) were observed in 2 subjects (33.3% in the series) whereas, Gaps (G) were observed in 3 subjects (50.0% in the series). Terminal deletions (TD) were observed in the sample of a single subject.

• • •

Conclusion

Present work attempted to study cytogenetic anomalies in poor academic children of Bhopal. This cytogenetic study was carried out with the selective sampling of a total of 122 subjects of the age group of 6 to 18 years, comprised of 56 persons (34 male and 22 female) who had mental sublevel hence exhibited poor academic performance and 52 persons (32 male and 20 females) who were normal, taken as control in the present study. Recruited children belonged to both urban as well as rural areas. Children from urban areas were 83.61% and rest 16.39% were from rural areas. Majority of subjects (92.86%) with mental sub-level were from urban settings and rest 7.14% were from rural areas. Majority of subjects were from middle class being at 34.43% followed by children belonging to Below Poverty line being at 26.59%. Furthermore, 21.31% children belonged to Lower-middle class children followed by Upper class children being at 19.67%.

It was observed in the present study that there were variable levels of intellectual disability in selective subjects with mental sub-level. Out of a total of 56 children recruited from this group, a majority being 21 had moderate intellectual disability (IQ 36-51) followed by 16 with mild intellectual disability (IQ 52-69) status. Furthermore, 13 children showed severe Intellectual disability (IQ 20- 35) and there were only 6 children who had profound intellectual disability (IQ 19 or below). The present study demonstrated frequency of chromosomal abnormalities in subjects with intellectual disability and control. Significantly higher 44.64% of subjects with intellectual disability showed varied chromosomal abnormalities as compared to the control group which showed 15.15%. Frequency was 29.49% higher in subjects with mental sub-level. In the control group, 84.84% of subjects showed normal karyotype being significantly higher as compared to subjects with mental sub-level which showed these to be 55.35%. The mean value of the aberrant metaphases in subjects with mental sub-level was 38.26 + 2.62 whereas, it was considerably low being 12.15 + 4.33 in normal control showing a statistically significant difference ($p<0.01$).

Gender-wise distribution in this revealed that 76% of male subjects and 24% of female subjects had chromosomal abnormalities. Both autosomal and sex chromosome abnormalities were observed. There were structural as well as numerical abnormalities of autosomes in the subjects investigated whereas, only structural abnormalities were found in the series of sex chromosome abnormalities. The majority of autosomal aberrations being 22 (88%) were structural in the series and only 1 (4%) showed numerical abnormality of autosomes being trisomy of 21 chromosomes in a male out of a total of 25 detected with different types of chromosome abnormalities. Structural sex chromosomal abnormalities were noted in 2 subjects comprising 1 male and 1 female. Normal karyotypes were also observed in 31 (55.35%) subjects who had intellectual disabilities. Frequencies of varied chromosome-type aberrations were lower in the control group comprised of normal children as compared to the group of subjects with intellectual disabilities. Chromosome-type aberrations involved ring chromosomes (44.4% in the series), dicentric chromosomes (22.2% in the series), and acrocentric associations (22.2% in the series). Similarly, chromatid-type aberrations in subjects with intellectual disability were lower in the control group comprised of normal children as compared to the group of subjects with intellectual disability. Chromatid-type aberrations involved chromatid breaks (53.3% in the series), Gaps (26.6% in the series), and Terminal deletions (20.0% in the series). In this series two samples with multiple-type aberrations involved chromatid-type abnormality.

Chromosomal abnormalities are an important cause of intellectual disability and their frequency increases with the severity of the intellectual disability. It is concluded that chromosomal studies in children with intellectual disability assist in accurate diagnosis and proper prognosis followed by genetic counseling and management rehabilitation. The magnitude of chromosomal abnormalities in children with Intellectual disabilities poses a serious health problem in our country and still requires further examination in diverse populations with varied socio-cultural features in future studies.

• • •

Bibliography

- Abraham, S. and Silva, F.D.(2014): Effectiveness Of Counseling On Quality Of Life Of Patients With Human Immunodeficiency Virus/ Acquired Immunodeficiency Syndrome In Selected Antiretroviral Therapy Centers Of Mangalore. *Asian Journal of Pharmaceutical and Clinical Research*, 1 (4):169-172.
- Alfirevic, Z., Mujezinovic, F., Sundberg, K. (2003): Amniocentesis and chorionic villus sampling for prenatal diagnosis. The Cochrane Database of Systematic Reviews, (3), CD003252. Advance online publication.
- Andrieux J, Dubourg C, Rio M, (2009): Genotype-phenotype correlation in four 15q24 deleted patients identified by array-CGH. Am J Med Genet;149A:2813-9.
- Annunziato, A. (2008): DNA Packaging: Nucleosomes and Chromatin. NatureEducation 1(1):26
- Blair, C. (2002): School readiness. Integrating cognition and emotion in a neurobiological conceptualization of children's functioning at school entry.
- Boat, T.F. and Wu, J.T. editors (2015): Mental Disorders and Disabilities Among Low-Income Children. Washington (DC): National Academics Press (US);. Am Psychol. 57(2):111-27
- Borgaonkar, D.S. (1997): Chromosomal Variation in Man: A Catalog of Chromosomal Variants and Anomalies (Eighth Edition). Wiley-Liss
- Boyle S., Brock, A., Mace, J. and Sibbons, M. (2002): Reaching the Poor: The 'Costs' of Sending Children to School. Synthesis Report. London: DFID.
- Brett, D., Pospisil, H., Valcarcel, J., Reich, J., & Bork, P. (2002): Alternative splicing and genome complexity. Nature Genetics, 30, 29–30.
- Brookwell, R: Daniel, A; Turner, G; Fishburn, J. (1982): The fragile X(q27)form of X- linked mental retardation: FudR as an inducing agent for frac(q27) expression in lymphocytes, fibroblasts, and amniocytes. AmJMed Genet, 13: 139-148.
- Burks, B. (1928): The relative influence of nature and nurture upon mental development: A comparative study on foster parent-foster child resemblance. Yearbook of the National Society for the Study

ofEducation, Part 1, 27, 219–316.

- Butler M.G; Meaney F.J; Palmer, C.G. (1986): Clinical and cytogenetic survey of39 individuals with Prader-Labhart-Willi syndrome. Am JMed Genet;23:793-809.
- Carrano, A. V; Thompson, L. H; Lindi, P. A; and Minckler, J. L. (1978): Sister chromatid exchange as an indicator of mutagenesis. Nature (Lond.),277:551-553.
- Census (2011): Govt. of India. Census 2011. Provisional Population Report. Office of the Registrar of Home General Affairs. and Census Commissioner India. Ministry Govt. of India: 2012. Available from:http://www.censusindia.gov.in
- Chakrabarti, S; Fombonne, E. (2001): Pervasive developmental disorders in preschool children. JAMA, 285:3093-9.
- Chipuer, H. M., Rovine, M. J., &Plomin, R. (1990). LISREL modeling: Genetic and environmental influences on IQ revisited. Intelligence, 14,11–29.
- Chipuer, H. M., Rovine, M. J., &Plomin, R. (1990). LISREL modeling: Genetic and environmental influences on IQ revisited. Intelligence, 14, 11–29.
- Chugh S. (2011): Dropout in Secondary Education A Study of ChildrenLivingin Slums of Delhi. Occasional 37; papers National University of Educational Planning and Administration (NUEPA), pp 1-41.
- Collins, F.S. (1992): Positional cloning: let's not call it reverse anymore. Nat Genet 1992; 1: 3–6.
- Deary, I. J; Spinath F.M; Bates T.C. (2006): Genetics of intelligence. European Journal of Human Genetics, 14, 690–700.
- Doll, Edgar A The Measurement of Social Competence: A Manual for the Vineland Social Maturity Scale1953 Minneapolis Educational Test Bureau (720 Washington Avenue, S. E.) 641
- Down, J. L. H. (1866): Observations on an Ethnic Classification of Idiots. London Hospital Reports, 3:259-262,
- Durkin, M.S; Wang, W; Shrout, P.E; Zaman, S.S; Hasan, Z.M; Desai P, et al. (1995): Evaluating a ten-question screen for childhood disability: Reliability and internal structure in different cultures. J. Clin. Epidemiol., 48:657-66.
- Eddy, S. R. (2001). Non-coding RNA genes and the modern RNA world. Nature Reviews Genetics, 2, 919–929.

- El-Hattab AW, Smolarek TA, Walker ME, et al. (2009): Redefined genomic architecture in 15q24 directed by patient deletion/ duplication breakpoint mapping. Hum Genet; 126:589-602. 77.
- Erlenmeyer-Kimling, L., &Jarvik, L. F. (1963). Genetics and intelligence: A review. Science, 142, 1477–1479.
- Evans K.L; Muir, W.J; Blackwood, D.H; Porteous, D.J. (2001): Nuts and bolts of psychiatric genetics: building on the Human Genome Project. Trends. Genet; 17: 35- 40.
- Falconer, D. S., & Mackay, T. F. C.(1996): Introduction to quantitative genetics, 4th ed. (London, Prentice-Hall, 1996.
- Fraga, Mario F.; Ballestar, Esteban (2005). "Epigenetic differences arise during the lifetime of monozygotic twins". Proc.Natl. Acad.Sci. U.S.A. 102 (30): 10604–9.
- Gallagher A and Hallahan B. (2012): Fragile X-associated disorders: a clinical overview. J Neurol., 259(3):401-413.
- Galton F. (1869): Hereditary genius: An inquiry into its laws and consequences. London, McMillan/Fontana (Reprinted in 1962).
- Galton, F. (1876): The history of twins as a criterion of the relative powers of nature and nurture. Royal Anthropological Institute of Great Britain and Ireland Journal, 6, 391–406.
- Glaser B, Hessl D, Dyer-Friedman J, et al. (2003): Biological and environmental contributions to adaptive behavior in FXS. Am J MedGenet A.;117A (1):21 –29.
- Gorlin, R.; Cohen M.M. Jr, Levin, L.S. (1990): Syndromes of the Head and Neck. New York, Oxford University Press.
- Gustafson, R; Wahlstrom, Johannisson, T; Holmqvist, D. (1991): Chromosomal aberrations in the mildly mentally retarded. J Men Defic Res; 35: 246- 246.
- Goswami, H.K; Chandorkar, M; Bhattacharya, K; Vaidyanath, G; Parmar, D; Sengupta, S; Patidar, S.L; Sengupta, L.K; Goswami, R. and Sharma, P.N. (1990): Search for chromosomal variations among gas-exposed persons in Bhopal. Hum. Genet., 84: 172-76.
- Gripenberg, U; Hongell, K; Knuutila, S; Kahkonen, M; Leisti, J. (1980): A chromosome survey of 1602 mentally retarded patients. Evaluation of a long-term study at the Rinnekoti Institution, Finland. - Hereditas 92: 223- 228. Hagerman, R.J. and Hagerman, P.J., editors. (2002): FXS: diagnosis,treatment,and research. Baltimore (MD): Johns Hopkins UniversityPress.

- Hernandez, L.M; Blazer, D.G; editors.(2006): Genes, Behavior, and the Social Environment: Moving Beyond the Nature/Nurture Debate. Washington (DC): National Academies Press (US).
- Hoggart, A; Wu, D; LaSalle, J.M; Schanen, N.C. (2010): The comorbidity of autism with the genomic disorders of chromosome 15qll.2-ql3. Neurobiol Dis;38:181-91.
- Hornby, A.S. (2000): Oxford advanced learners dictionary of current English. Oxford, UK. Oxford University Press.
- Hsu, T. C. (1952): Mammalian chromosomes in vitro I: The karyotype of man. Journal of Heredity, 43: 167-172.
- Hunter A.G.W. (2002): Medical genetics: The diagnostic approach to the child with dysmorphic signs. CMAJ; 167(4):367-72.
- Hunter, N. and May, J. (2003): Poverty, Shocks and School DisruptionEpisodes among Adolescents in South Africa. CSDS Working Paper,No.35.
- Advisor(SecondEdition). Instant Diagnosis and Treatment. Edited In Pediatric Clinical
- Hyman, S.L. (2007): Mental retardation. by:Lynn C.Garfunkel, Jeffrey M. Kaczorowski, and Cynthia Christy.
- ISCN (1985): An International System for Human Cytogenetic Nomenclature,1985, Report of the Standing Committee on Human CytogeneticNomenclature, Published in collaboration with 'Cytogenetics and CellGenetics'. Karger Publications.
- ISCN (1995): An International System for Human Cytogenetic Nomenclature: Recommendations of the International Standing Committee on HumanCytogenetic Nomenclature, Memphis, Tenn., October 1994Published in collaboration with 'Cytogeneticsand Cell Genetics'Eds.: Mitelman F. (Lund).
- Jayaprakash, R (2005): Diagnostic Profile In Children Presenting With PoorAcademic Performance—A Clinic-Based Study. IACAM nationalconference, Lucknow.
- Kamat, V. V. (1934): A revision of the Binet scale for Indian children (Kanarese and Marathi speaking). Br J Edu Psychol.;4:296-309.
- Kanner L.(1943): Autistic disturbances of affective contact. Nervous Child 2, 217- 250.
- Indian J.Pediatr., Karande S., Kulkarni M (2005): Poor school performance. 72(11):961-967.
- Kavita Singh, C.B.S. Dangi and Dinesh Parmar (2018 a). Cytogenetic

Anomalies in Poor Academic Children. SHODH SANGAM, 1, No.01, 74-79.

- Kavita Singh, Dinesh Parmar and CBS Dangi (2018 b): Genetic basis of pooracademicperformance among children: A review. Biosci. Biotech.Res. Comm. (BBRC), 11(4): 766-772.
- Kavita Singh, Shadma Siddiqui and CBS Dangi (2019): Chromosomal Abnormalities in Children with Poor Academic Performance. Biosci.Biotech. Res. Comm. (BBRC), Vol 12 No (1) Jan-Mar 2019.
- Kearsey, M. J. (1998): The principles of QTL analysis (a minimalmathematicsapproach). Journal of Experimental Botany 49, 1619 –1623 Lynch, M., &Walsh, B. Genetics and Analysis of QuantitativeTraits (Sunderland,MA, Sinauer, 1998.
- Khurana S. (1980): Non–intellectual factors in learning disability. Indian Journal of Psychiatry, 22: 256-260.
- Klopocki E, Graul-Neumann LM, Grieben U, et al. (2008): A further case oftherecurrent 15q24 microdeletion syndrome, detected by array CGH.Eur JPediatr;167:903-8.
- Klopocki E, Graul-Neumann LM, Grieben U, et al. (2008): A further case oftherecurrent 15q24 microdeletion syndrome, detected by array CGH.Eur JPediatr 167:903-8.
- inversion polymorphism. Nat Genet; 38: 999-1001. with associated syndrome a common
- Koolen, D,A; Vissers, L.E; Pfundt, R, (2006): A new chromosome 17q21.31 microdeletion
- Lakhan, R; Ekúndayò, O. T; Shahbazi, M. (2015). An estimation of the prevalence of intellectual disabilities and their association with age in rural and urban populations in India. Journal of Neurosciences in Rural Practice, 6(4), 523–528.
- Lejeune, J; Gautier, M; Turpin, R. (1959): Etudes dcs chromosomessomatiquedc neuf cnfants mongoliens. CR Hebd Seances Acad Sci;248:1721-
- Lubs, H. A. (1969): A marker X chromosome. Am. J. Hum. Genet, 21: 231 -244.
- Lucassen, R., Coulter, D. L., Holloway, E. A., Reiss, S., Schalock, R. L., Snell, classification, and systems of supports (9th Edition).Washington, DC: American
- M. E., Spitalnick, D. M., & Stark, J. A. (1992): Mental retardation:Definition, Association on Mental Retardation.

- Lucy Raymond, F. and Tarpey, P.(2006): The genetics of mental retardation. Human Molecular Genetics, 15(l): 110-116.
- Malt, EA; Dahl, RC; Haugsand, TM; Ulvestad, IH; Emilsen, NM; Hansen, B;Cardenas, YE; Skøld, RO; Thorsen, AT; Davidsen, EM (2013): Healthand disease in adults with Down syndrome. Tidsskr Nor Legeforen nr.133 (3): 290–294.
- McClearn, G. E. (1963). The inheritance of behaviour. In L. J. Postman (Ed.), Psychology in the making (pp. 144–252). New York: Knopf.
- McKusick, V.A. (1978): Human Genetics (2nd Edition). Prentice-Hall ofIndiaP vt. Ltd., New Delhi. P. 95.
- Mefford, H.C; Batshaw, M.L; Hoffman, E.P. (2012): Genomics, IntellectualDisability, and Autism. N Engl J Med; 366(8):733-743.
- Mercer, J. R. (1973): Labeling the Mentally Retarded, Review. Berkeley, Calif.: University of California Press, p. 332.
- Miele F. (2002): What is intelligence? In: intelligence, race, and genetics. Oxford, UK.Westview Press.
- Mogasale, V.V; Patil, V.D; Patil, N.M; Mogasale, V. (2012): Prevalence of specific learning disabilities among primary school children in a South Indian city. Indian J Pediatr.;79:342-7.
- Moghe, M: Patel, Z.M; Peter, J.J; Ambani. L.M. (1981): Cytogenetic studied in a selected group of mentally retarded children. Hum Genet; 58:184- 187.
- Moorhead, P.S; Nowell, P.L; Mellman, W.J; Battips, D.M; Hunaford, D.A.(1960):Chromosome preparation of leukocyte culture from humanperipheralblood. Exp. Cell. Res. 20: 613-616.
- Mukherjee, M; Shignapure, V. (2016): Challenges Faced By Parent Due Tothe Presence of Mentally Handicapped Person in the Family. TheInternational Journal of Indian Psychology, 3, Issue 3, No.2: 61-78.
- Natarajan, A.T. and Obe, G. (1980): Screening of human populations formutations induced by environmental pollutants: Use of humanlymphocyte system. Ecotoxicol Environ Saf. 4(4):468–481.
- Nouwens, P. J. G., Lucas, R., Smulders, N. B. M., Embregts, P. J. C. M., & van Nieuwenhuizen, C. (2017): Identifying classes of persons with mild intellectual disability or borderline intellectual functioning: a latent class analysis. BMC Psychiatry, 17, 257-264.
- O'Sullivan, R. J., and Karlseder, J. (2010): Telomeres: protecting chromosomes againstgenome instability. Nature Reviews. Molecular Cell Biology, 11(3), 171– 181.

- Okoye, N. N. (1982). Why students fail examinations: Psychology foreverydayliving; A Nigeria Journal of Applied Psychology 11(2): 1 – 5.
- Patterson D (2009): Molecular genetic analysis of Down 126(1):195-214. syndrome. HumGenet
- Penrose, L. S. (Lionel Sharples) (1938): A clinical and genetic study of 1280 cases of mental defect. H. M. Stationery off, London.
- Perez Jurado, L.A; Peoples, R; Kaplan, P; Hamel, B.C; Francke, U. (1996):Molecular definition of the chromosome 7 deletion in Williamssyndrome and parent-of-origin effects on growth. Am J Hum Genet;59:781-92.
- Plomin R and Spinath FM. (2004): Intelligence: genetics, genes, andgenomics. Journal of Personality and Social Psychology. 86 (1), 112-129.
- Plomin, R., DeFries, J. C., McClearn, G. E., & McGuffin, P. (2001):Behavioralgenetics (4th ed.). New York: Worth Publishers.
- Pratinidhi, A.K, Kurulkar, P.V; Garad, S.G; Dalal, M. (1992):Epidemiologicalaspects of school dropouts in children between 7 – 5years in ruralMaharashtra. Indian J Pediatr 59:423-7.
- Raver, C.C. (2002); Emotions matter: Making the case for the role of youngchildren's emotional development for early school readiness. SocialPolicy Report, Society for Research in Child Development. 16:3–18.
- Raymond, F. L. (2006). X linked mental retardation: a clinical guide. Journal of Medical Genetics, 43(3), 193–200.
- Raynham, H; Gibbons, R; Flint, J; Higgs, D. (1996): Review The genetic basis for mental retardation. QJ Med; 89:169-175
- Reddy, V.B; Gupta, A; Lohiya, A, Kharya, P..(2013): Mental health issues and challenges in India. IJSER, 3:1-3.
- Reschly, D.J; Myers, T.G; Hartel, C.R. editors (2002): Mental Retardation: Determining Eligibility for Social Security Benefits, National Research Council (US) Committee on Disability Determination for Mental Retardation; Washington (DC): National Academies Press (US).
- Restivo L, Ferrari F, Passino E, et al. (2005): Enriched environment promotesbehavioural and morphological recovery in a mouse model for the FXS.Proc Natl Acad Sci U S A;102 (32):11557–11562.
- Ropers, H. H. (2008): Genetics of intellectual disability. Curr Opin GenetDev;18: 241- 50.
- Sarason, S. B. (1949). Psychological problems in mental deficiency.

Oxford, England: Harper.

- Satya-Murti, S; Cohen, B.H; Michelson, D. (2013): Chromosomal MicroarrayAnalysis for Intellectual Disabilities. American academy of Neurology
- Schalock, R.L; Luckasson, R.A; Shogren, K.A; Borthwick-Duffy, S; BradleyV;Buntinx, W.H.E., et al. (2007): The renaming of retardation:Understanding the change to the term intellectual mental disability. IntellectDevDisabil. 45(2):116-24.
- Seabright M. (1971): A rapid banding technique for human chromosome. Lancet. II: 971-972.
- Sharma, A.K. and Sharma, A. (1980) Chromosome Techniques: Theory and Practice. Butterworths,
- Sharma S, Raina S. K, Bhardwaj A. K, Chaudhary S, Kashyap V, Chander V. (2016): Prevalence of mental retardation in urban and rural populations of the goitre zone in Northwest India. Indian J Public Health; 60:131 - 137.
- Sharp, A.J; Hansen, S; Selzer, R.R. (2006): Discovery of previouslyunidentified genomic disorders from the duplication architecture of the human genome. Nat Genet;38:1038-42.
- Shaw-Smith C. Pittman A.M. Willatt L. (2006): Microdeletion encompassingMAPT at chromosome 17q21.3 is associated with developmental delayand learning disability. Nat Genet; 38:1032-7.
- Simmons, D. (2008) Genetic inequality: Human genetic engineering. Nature Education 1(1):173-186.
- Simonoff. E; Bolton, P; Rutter, M. (1996): Mental retardation: Genetic findings, clinical implications and research agenda. J Child Psychol Psychiat 1996; 37: 259- 280.
- SiqueiraI, C. M. and Gurge-Giannetti, J. (2011). Poor school performance: anupdated review. Revista da Associação Médica Brasileira, 5(1): 78 -86.
- Smith, A.C; McGavran, L; Robinson, J. (1986): Interstitial deletion of(17)(all.2pll.2) in nine patients. Am J Med Genet; 24:393 -414.
- Smith, G.F.. and Warren, S.T. (1985): The Biology of down Syndrome. Acad Sci. ;450:1-9.
- Stafford, R. L. and Meyer, R.J. (1968): Diagnosis and Counseling Of The Mentally Retarded: Implications For School Health. Journal of School Health, 38(3): 151-155. Blackwell Publishing Ltd.
- Sucuoğlu, Esen and Alkoç, Gülçiçek. (2017): The Examination of

Anthropometric Measurements of Children with Mental Disabilities and Normal Development. International Journal of Scientific Study. 5: 110-117.

- Sutherland, G. R. (1982a): Heritable fragile sites on human chromosomes.Vlll.Preliminary population cytogenetic data onthe folic-acid- sensitivefragile sites. Am. J. Hum. Genet, 34: 452-158.
- Sutherland. G. R. (1982b): Heritable fragile sites on human chromosomes, IX.Population cytogenetic and segregation analysis of the BrdU-requiring fragile site at 10q25. Am. J. Hum. Genet, 34: 753-756.
- Tarjan G. (1965): The role ofthe primary physician in mental retardation. Calif Med; 102:419-425.
- Terman, L. M. and Merrill, M. A. (1937): Measuring Intelligence: A Guide to the Administration of the New Revised Stanford-Binet Tests of Intelligence. Boston Houghton Mifflin Co461
- Thapar, A. (2013): Copy Number Variation: What Is It and What Has It Told Us About Child Psychiatric Disorders? J Am Acad Child Adoles Psychiatry,52(8): 772– 774.
- Thompson, J.S. and Thompson, M.W. (1986): Genetics in Medicine. W.B Saunders Co., Philadelphia, Pennsylvania.
- Tredgold, A. F., and Soddy, K. 1956. A textbook of mental deficiency. 9th ed.
- Baltimore: Williams & Wilkins. Turnpenny, P.D. and Ellard, S. editors (2017): Emery's Elements of MedicalGenetics 15th Edition. Elsevier
- UNICEF (2011): The Situation of Children in India. A Profile. UNICEF.
- Valente, M. (1972): Counseling parents of retarded children. Calif Med 116:21- 26.
- Valiente, C., Swanson, J., & Eisenberg, N. (2012). Linking Students'Emotionsand Academic Achievement: When and Why EmotionsMatter. ChildDevelopment Perspectives, 6(2), 129–135.
- Vignal, A., (2002): A review on SNP and other types of molecular markersandtheir use in animal genetics. Genetics Selection Evolution 34, 275 –305.
- Warkany, J; Lemire, R.I; Cohen, M.M. (1981): Jr. Mental Retardation and Congenital Malformations of the Central Nervous System. Chicago, Year Book Medical Publishers.
- WHO (1968): Organization of services for the mentally retarded: fifteenth report of the WHO Expert Committee on Mental Health [meeting held in Geneva from 26 September to 2 October 1967].

Authors: WHO Expert Committee on Mental Health · World Health Organization. Issue Date: 1968. Publisher: Geneva: World Health

- WHO (1975): The International Conference for the Ninth Revision of the International Statistical Classification of Diseases, Injuries, and Causes of Death, convened by WHO, met in Geneva from 30 September to 6 October 1975.
- Willemsen, R., Levenga, J., and Oostra, B. A. (2011): CGG repeats inthe FMR1gene: size matters. Clinical Genetics, 80(3), 214–225.
- Yasseen, A.K. and Al-Musawi, T.A. (2001): Cytogenetics study in severely mentally retarded patients. Neurosciences 6 (3): 156-161.
- Zhu, J (2011): Genetic counselling and birth defect prevention. Paper presented at the National conference on early pregnancy and prenatal screening and birth defect prevention, Kunming, Yunnan Province, C.

• • •

Contributors

Dr. Kavita Singh

Dr. Kavita Singh (Co-author)

Dr. Kavita Singh, Asst. prof. Pentium Point Technical College, APS University, Rewa) completed her research in Biotechnology and she was a project in-charge for a period of five yrs () on Sickle Cell sponsored by M. P. Council of Science and Technology.

• • •

Dr. S.D. Singh

Dr. S. D. Singh (illustrate)

Dr. S.D. Singh, Prof and Head, Department of Botany, Geetanjali Govt. Degree College, Bhopal. He has working experience in the Higher Education Govt. of M P and M P Private University Regulatory Commission. He supervised 07 researcher scholars for Ph.D. awards.

• • •

Prof. Shadma Siddiqui

Prof. Shadma Siddiqui (Editor)

Prof. Shadma Siddiqui, Dean, School of Paramedical Sciences, SAM Global University, Raisen, MP. She has 18 years of Academic Excellence in Life Sciences, Paramedical Sciences, and Forensic Sciences and has expertized in the broad fields of Allied Sciences and Medical Technology, Clinical Nutrition, Biotechnology, Molecular Biology, Forensic Science, Medical Microbiology, Industrial and Applied Microbiology. She was awarded as a Best Women Academician in 2022. She is a reviewer, editor, and regular writer of scientific magazines. She supervised students for dissertations, internships, and training in applied areas. She has authored 03 books, numerous research papers, articles, etc.

• • •

www.ingramcontent.com/pod-product-compliance
Ingram Content Group UK Ltd.
Pitfield, Milton Keynes, MK11 3LW, UK
UKHW021924190726
13853UKWH00002B/828